GOD PICKED ME

Gayle,

Blessings

Bonnie 2025

A Publication of Tall Pine Books
|| tallpinebooks.com

*Printed in the United States of America

GOD PICKED ME

GOD, ME, AND MY SURVIVAL THROUGH CANCER

BONNIE J. SCHAAL

Tall Pine

This book can only be dedicated to my best friend, GOD.

SPECIAL THANKS

To all whom I have loved: My boy, daughter number 1, daughter number 2, my ex, and my ever so patient S O (Soulmate)! He stood by me through tough, rough, sad, happy, mean, and kind. He is always loving and is still by my side, holding my heart in his wonderful, powerful hands. I love you, always, ME.

CONTENTS

PART III

PREFACE

To know who you are is one of the greatest joys a human life can have. To know where you are, even better! Keeping true to yourself is your survival path in this long journey called life. Your heart will always lead you. Your mind will play tricks. Your own instincts have the power to prevail. Learn to use all of these and keep moving up. Move up to the greatest power of all, your own personal love of God.

PART I

1

My reason for this book is to show God as good, funny, and true. God started out building the earth, saying, "Let there be light." God made man, then He made woman from man's rib. Through them came life, children, and family. Then came sin, conflict, unrest, and all human concepts. Through it all, God remained constant, steadfast, and true. I know it's hard to understand, and not everyone can or will choose to. We all have our own life to explore, maneuver, and be guided through. We can understand it. If you let Him, He does show you how to work and find your own path. Take the left, center, or right; *you* have that choice.

As God has shown so many times, we (as humans) haven't really changed from the beginning. We have always been given free will, and that is our true course. We are the only ones who know which family we belong to. In my path, I was told by my mom, "I have champagne taste" and "was not part of the Rockefellers," and "I was born into the wrong family." I always wanted more and better. I was really creating my own path. It didn't fit into my born-family values, really! Now that I'm older, it's okay.

But growing up, what turmoil it presented! I guess it affected my parents also. So I did my best to create my journey. My path really started as a 16 year old, when I fell madly in love. I had my first boyfriend, my first real boyfriend! I had boys I liked when I was younger, but this was a real boyfriend. This was it, a real true love. Not knowing how this worked, I only had trial and error. So I proceeded and did what I was shown—love, marriage, children, and family—all the time, hoping it all went as planned. Being young, stupid, and naïve, I believed, as they say, that love would conquer all. So this was the beginning for me.

2
_____

All your life, you try to do the right thing. Isn't is so sad, that so many people (because you let them) put strains on you? Thinking you found the right person and things happen? Promises made and promises broken? It leads to feeling that one day (maybe), you'll find him. You try so many times and come back to the same conclusion: you only have yourself. Make your own way, curses to those who hold you back! The bottom line is, you let them.

Life makes you think you can't be by yourself. But guess what, you can! Right now, I'm sitting at a friend's pool. She and her husband are at work. I am left in her backyard playing with Stella (what I call her), her Polaris pool cleaner. She gets caught and I pull her away from the metal stairs on the side of the pool. She gets caught again and the game continues. She's winning! My point is, who cares! Feeling this: done, it's great, no demands, no conflict. I only have my boombox radio, my cd's, soda, water, and a salad. What a great day to make myself content, something no one else can do. Thank you, God, for giving me this right!

I found it cosmic, all four corners around me: north, south, east, and west. All mine were these corners of the world. Everything at my disposal. What more could a person ask for? Life is great. Love that other thing, take it for what it is. So many songs on the radio tell you about everyone's life. Have you ever really listened to the words? Think about it. How many times have you heard a song and it puts your life right before you? One of mine is a Kid Rock,/Cheryl Crow song called "Picture." Where was that about 30 years ago? I could have used it back then.

I grew up in New Jersey—what a great state! I love the east coast. There's nothing better for me. I've started reading the Janet Evanovich book series (16 or so books). Stephanie Plum is the star. It takes me back to New Jersey, knowing all those great places and reading about them. So many of my pals have read them. We're always getting more to read, fun facts to learn. Fast and funny, a no-brainer. In this troubled world, what a great way to pass dead time. I miss my solitude time around my pool from the big house in New Jersey (we used to call it the Ponderosa). I now live on the Chesapeake in Maryland, also a great place, but miss the big NJ. It became a leaving-get-out-of-dodge thing. But we all do what we have to. Just a little more background before I go on. Am I really ready to write a book about, "what do you call it, Life?"

You wake up one day and you're here on earth. How did you get here? Parents. Do they really care about each other? Most likely once upon a time, but now you wonder what made them so mad about everything. You learn as you get older that you get the brain you were born with. It all starts to work and show you what happens to people who use it. The real smarts that you were taught and how to use it or how not to use it. I prefer to use it! Maybe I didn't like it all the time, but...we learn it's a good thing. The more we learn, the more confused we can make ourselves.The best is to just keep getting the knowledge to go on. Find one, maybe two topics and run with it. Make it good, do your best, learn everything well, and *become* you! The best person you can become is you, finding your real self. Do it for yourself. Forget about everyone else, because really down deep, they could care less. But you love yourself, more than anyone else does, so remember you are important. People forget to tell each other that, and when it's too late, then they remember. I should have... too late!

You see, this all leads up to a story I would like to tell. She was born in New Jersey to her parents, two people she always thought loved each other beyond love. She was the third child, second girl (then another boy, girl, girl). Six children, four girls, two boys, in a lower middle class family. She didn't know she was lower class until she got into sixth grade. They moved to a new neighborhood, new school, and met so many new people. That's when she realized people had so much more, and she wanted it. Remember, I said lower middle class. She thought she must think of a way to get the higher level. Being naïve, she thought, "No big deal. I can do this."

The reality was, it isn't that easy. It was going to take hard work and getting to know the correct people. So she started to find them. But as she did, she encountered many people who could have cared less about her. What a realization that scared her to no end! She thought she finally found her new friendships in ninth grade (this was in the '60s). Times were so different then; costs were much cheaper to our standards of today. At that time, it all seemed expensive. Thinking she'd found her confidantes, she confided so many of her life secrets to them, her friends. By Monday morning back at school, the secrets were out. Every one of them. And everyone around the school was talking. She could hardly believe her ears! Not that anything was bad. But they were her secrets.

That was a very hard lesson to learn at such a young age (15). Thinking that she could trust. Hurt by the people, pals, girlfriends *she thought* she could trust. Learning you can't. Thinking back on it, she realized it had been that way her short-long life and she was unaware. Understand the concept; she now is 15, and she wouldn't do that again. Don't expect that to happen from her so-called friends. She became everyone's friend: no clicks, no best friends, no more in a crowd. That doesn't always work, either; if you're not with the in-crowd, you're not in at all. She came to realize, better to be friends with everyone than with no one. So all through high school, this was how it was. She did her own thing. She rode horses, but couldn't afford her own. She became their friend, never letting one person come too close. She made the friendship rules.

It became very real for her. She blossomed into a really great friend and trustworthy person. She always told herself that if someone told her something in confidence, she'd go to the grave with it, no matter what. It became one of her golden rules she cherished about herself. In time, people came to realize you could be her best friend. She kept her secrets and yours to herself. She always befriended the new kid/person in school or town. She made them feel welcome and introduced them around. Usually, she was the one who was left out. She did not care. She kept on her way and did what she felt was right *for herself*. She kept on the course of life, she put forth herself. It made her very happy to see that she could be a small part of someone else's life to help them feel they were happy along their way. She always felt she was born to do this, that God gave her a special gift to be helpful every which way she could. She prevailed in her steady life. She loved so many things. She was becoming that young woman who was going to be responsible for herself, and she learned to love.

In this becoming, she started letting herself open up to the many trials of life again. She met her soon-to-be husband at age 17, falling madly in love. She could not seem to let go. They soon married (when she was 20) and thought life had given her the best thing she had ever been through. It was a long courtship, her parents demanded it. Looking back on it, it was a good thing. When people tell you, "You're too young," listen to them. Get to know someone, and learn about yourself.

The marriage went off as planned. It was a great wedding! Everyone talked about it for years. The day was so cold with a snowy blizzard. The sun shone brightly, and it warmed up slightly to keep everyone in the festive mood. Food and cake couldn't have been tastier! She couldn't believe that day had come, her dream come true.

She married the man she loved so. Within nine months, they bought their first house and life was wonderful.

Within two years of marriage, they had their first child, a boy named after his father and many generations before him. It's always a great thing to know your child can carry on a family tradition, with a name that has been in your family for over 100 years. Soon another child, 2 ½ years later, and you have the ideal family; a girl, a daddy's girl, you gave him what he wanted. The perfect family: daddy, mommy, boy, and girl. All the perfect things that could happen, did. You go on thinking, "I'm the luckiest person in the world. Life couldn't be better." You say, "Thank You, God," so many times. You become a stay-at-home mom. You take your children to preschool, have play dates, and meet other great moms.

3

All this time, you are looking and watching. Seeing how others live and looking at yourself. I had a wonderful life! Or so I thought. Things always look great from the outside. But as the saying goes, "When the doors and windows are closed," things go from bad to worse. I thought I was untouchable, and my worst nightmare blew up in my face. The tornado hits! I am again alone, feeling the hits. They just keep getting fuller, longer, and more explosive. Years have passed, and I've kept it together for the good of the family. At least, that is what I thought.

Months and years go by. The phone rings, suspicions raging, women calling, paging, late nights at the office ,and dinner dates. Only they were with other women. Betrayal. I can't even tell you how to explain the pain that a betrayal can cause. People tell you they are your lovers, friends, and family. They only want what they want. They are too focused on themselves, not about helping you ease your pain. Since you still want what's best, you try to keep things even. Where do you go for help? No one can help. Nobody cares. Not even the family or in-laws you think are yours. Can you believe your mother-in-law saying, "I did it; it's your turn!" Shock!

A huge realization floods your senses that you are alone. It is only you and the betrayals begin. Okay, grasp it, remember who you are! You're better than they are. Smarter than they are. Quicker than they are. You have your kids to think of. Get it together! All the time, you're screaming inside. To make matters worse, you are pregnant with number three. You know in your mind, it's another girl. You also know in your mind that you can't have another boy. The husband could only handle one.

4

ENCOUNTER # 1

Six months prior, you had this dream.
August 1982

Y ou are a little girl sitting at the bended knee of Jesus. He's in His white robes, glowing and smiling, telling you, "You will have another child. A girl. She will be fine, always fine, never forget that. Your pregnancy, not so. Many perils, sickness, but remember the baby will always be fine. All the problems are with your human body. It may seem the baby's in stress, but it's your body, not the baby."

She says, "No" to Jesus.

He says, "I will protect them both, and not another pregnancy will happen after this one. But you must accept these terms."

I try to fight Him, but I know I can't. I wake up the next

morning and I can't believe I had this dream. I wake up crying and almost paralyzed. I can't move. All I can do is remember the dream.

5

The truth is, I can't do this, not again. My pregnancies are not great and I'm always sick, tired, and can't eat. Time marches on and my IUD (birth control) is causing problems. My body starts rejecting it and I'm bleeding all the time. By December 1982, my doctor says it must come out. So it does, and he gives me a diaphragm. This did not work on child number 2; it keeps flipping upside down. The doctor says if I did get pregnant, I most likely would end up losing the baby. Everything inside of me is so wide open. He does not see how things can stay inside.

I'm only thinking of the dream—what I was told—and I know better. This is really going to happen. At this point, I must believe God. My thoughts are going everywhere. Oh God, why me? Why do I have to go through this? Even with my knowing better, tests in February, March, April 1983 came back negative. In my mind, I know better. My body does, too.

Finally, I go to my little boy's first communion in May 1983. I am so sick; I have a bladder infection and the pain is unbearable. I call the doctor. I go see him for an ultrasound, and there she is. Three months along! So here I go, through all these tests. I have explained my circumstances to my doctor. The cheating, the perfume, and the deceit. The tests begin, STD tests, and the cosmic crisis starts. It came on like lightning, not letting up for six months. In July, the Braxton Hicks start and hospital stays began. The pills to keep her. Ridhidreen, is a new drug, and I'm also with no weight gain. Shaking all the time, the explosions, the fights, the name calling, "you're a hypochondriac!" Still, all the women haven't stopped calling. The lies, the deceit, and the whys. I can't do this now. Not ever.

God, God, oh why? How do I cope? I have two other children, and a cheating husband. Not allowed to do anything but lie in bed with my feet up. The fighting got worse since he had to help with the kids, the house, and the meals, none of which he wants to do. This goes on for months. Labor Day weekend is around the corner, and I go into labor. This time, it's real. Oh, my God, too soon, not good, help me. Back to the hospital. My husband is mad, beyond mad! He has to take time to make arrangements for the kids and five more days at the hospital.

I stayed in labor and delivery. Everyone has their babies and I just lay there. He visits, but all he does is get mad at me, calling me "the hypo." Finally, my doctor hears him and can't believe the things he's saying, and tells him to leave. Really kicks him out. Tells him, "If you can't step up, don't come back." Finally, someone tells him where to go. Deep inside, I'm smiling. "Give it to him," I think. He is a home-wrecker, wacko, the selfish one (ME, ME, ME ME, all he cares about). My senses go wild, and I'm finally able to calm down.

I got myself through and healed enough to go home. My other children were waiting for me. They could only see me through the window of my room, third floor of the hospital from the parking lot. Remember, this is the '80s, children were not allowed to visit. I get well enough to go home again, but I'm not allowed to do anything. Just rest, be calm, and pray.

All the time, I'm remembering my dream. It's not the baby; she is fine. The fighting begins again: "You are lazy," "Get up and do something", "You are just a hypo." Well, my strength is even broader now. I tell myself, "Just tune him out, take yourself back, get through this."

Two months go by: all the drugs and rest, and he starts with not coming home. In late October 1983, I feel I have gone long enough in this pregnancy. I take myself off all the drugs and tell the doctors I am done. I'm driving, going back to my life, she is old enough to survive if she is born. So it goes, I took my life back! My diet was strict and I gained 18 pounds.

She decided to be 13 days late. They told me she has gotten big and they didn't know what to expect. With all of my bleeding, drugs, and stress, she could be deformed, born without limbs, etc. My water broke. My husband is pissed he has to come home. Told me, he has a dinner meeting. Really? Must be a date. I make arrangements for the other two children. It's now about 6:30pm, and the kids are fed, content, and happy. They are going to have a baby sister. He comes home, gets me to the hospital, brings his male friend (again, really?). It's almost 9 pm by the time we get to the hospital. By 11 pm, I am in labor and he is mad as hell. It's taking too long. Says he has to go, he needed to take his friend home. I could not believe my ears. So I say, "Go, get out!" After he leaves, I begin to sob. Nurses, doctors, everyone who came in my room were horrified.

The night begins, the contractions were strong, long, and painful. Finally, at 3:37am she is born on a Friday morning. The staff helps me push her out, literally pushing on my stomach! She is perfect, exactly what God said, "My body, not the baby." Again, God is in total control. The hospital wanted to call her dad, and I say, "NO. He'll figure it out." They tell me I have to, hospital rules. They get the phone number, since I refused to give it to them. They bring a phone to my recovery bedside, dial the number, hand me the receiver. He answered, I say, "It's a girl," and hang up. Nine and a half hours and a tubal ligation, something he refused to sign for. Times changed and I didn't need his signature. He signed, madder than hell, saying that I was ruining everything." As God told me, no more pregnancies… I was done.

It's 5 am in the morning before I sleep. I finally fell asleep, and shortly after the light in my room goes on. I wake up to his voice, all happy and excited that there is a new baby girl in our family. He shows up all happy and excited at 6:30am! Tells the nurse to bring her to the room with him. Are you kidding me? I tell the nurse to show her to him and take her back to the nursery. I tell him to leave, I need my sleep. He had his, it's my turn. Shocked, but he did.. Didn't hear or see him until after 7pm that evening.

Getting my thoughts together for the visit, I just focus on taking care of me.

Daughter number two is with me when he walks in. All smiles with flowers, he acts like the proud papa. Which he was, but he looks at me and says, "You're still fat." I ignore his insults and am proud God remains with my family. He protects me and daughter number 2 from the foul mouth of this human.

Days later, I'm out of the hospital (as my sister-in-law, who has been watching my other two children, comes to pick us up at the hospital), and I'm back at home with my other two children. They are so happy to have a baby sister! My son says that she is his. Elated, this 8 year old wants to have his baby in his arms. On the sofa, he bonds, holding her, loving her, and she is his. Life doesn't get easier, but my children are safe, secure, and healthy.

Time has a way of helping to cope, so you do. Things didn't change much. But God's promise, I can accept.

6

Many years passed: things changed, we changed, built a new house, and bought a new business. The reality always came back. The drinking, partying, women, and staying away had started. From Thursday through Sunday or Monday, it only gets worse. He decides he's going to stay away almost all weekends.

I decided, after many years (8 to be exact), to get a divorce. It is now August 5th, 1990. I refer to it as "The War of the Roses." Back and forth to court, countless times. Two and a half years later, April 1, 1992 (April Fool's day), my divorce is final. It takes its toll, but I *know* it has to be done. Not just for me, but for my children, as well.

I feel as if I am dying, internally, really. I'm shaking all the time. I get sick. This has to end. We don't leave friends, he wants nothing to do with the girls (just too much to write). Hard, but in the end, I felt good about myself. I do some dating, and he has me followed: threats, real threats.

I decided to move out of state. The children are getting older and are in their teen years. Boy stays (first child). Girl #1 stays. Girl #2 (the youngest) comes with me. This was not without a struggle and threats, but at the last minute, 11 pm at night, he gives in as I say, "You sign the papers, or she stays with you." Everything is packed, the truck ready to pull out of the driveway. The house is sold and we both know full well he doesn't want her.

A few years passed; the older two children stayed in New Jersey. Every once in a while, he decided he wanted to see daughter #2. We took a drive to New Jersey, so she can have time with her father. It is now time for daughter #1 to graduate high school, and the ex-husband has gotten remarried. He has a new child, and the new Mrs. wants nothing to do with any of my three children.

Things hadn't changed. He was still an alcoholic and philanderer, and always was. Cheated on his new family. The phone calls hadn't stopped. Drunk, he wants my opinion. This usually happened at 3am in the morning! I disliked giving it, because I knew his routine, it didn't change. I told him as I always did, "God will only let you get away with this for so long."

In 1998, my ex-husband (at the age of 46) died of liver complications and a heart attack. My children were devastated, as kids would be. He had another young child, a girl. So it happened. God was in control. It has taken years for everyone to deal with this loss, some better than others. But we have all moved on. The son married with two children, a boy and a girl. Daughter number one married: also with two children, a boy and a girl! Daughter number two was single.

Life has been good. I found the best keeper ever! He is my rock, joy, and an honest man. "God gives as good as He takes."

7

In the interim of all these life lessons, God has shown me many things. I've talked about love, hate, family, and friends; but the most important is yourself—how you understand your own life lessons and how to deal with them. I've had many encounters with life, like getting that gut feeling something was good. The heart wrenching/knowing or feeling something was really bad. In me, I learned to roll with it or squash it. Many times, it came back to bite me in the ass, hard! When it did, either own it or dismiss it. I've done and still do both.

We are human. Our minds are our own to choose. So we do. Maybe, we think, I shouldn't have gone that way. I need to change it. We think that was the only way, or the correct way. Either way it was (what was done) your way. You may go back and change it. If you say you're sorry and cool the hot water, or stand and be out in the cold (either way), it's your path. Only you know the feeling of your situation. Good or bad, you can live with your decision or change the outcome.

In my reasoning, I've tried to look to the sky and see my light. I prayed to heaven, asked for mercy, help, and guidance; not always getting my way in answers. I realized the consequences that may loom—some do and did. Reflecting, maybe some still do! There are always lessons to be learned. I can point out a few to get me back to point. I've already told you about pregnancy number three, encounter number one, the dream. Which all have come true. To this day, I still have a hard, but wonderful love of all of it and I Thank You, Jesus.

This other one is profound, but an eye opener, as well: going through my divorce. It was long and hard with many complications toward the middle. I was dating, back and forth to the attorney, struggling, working, fighting with my ex, raising my children. I just had this overwhelming feeling of, "Why am I doing this? I should just give up.

8

ENCOUNTER # 2

May 1993

Going to bed that evening, I just was so overwhelmed that I thought I should die. Remove me from this hell! But God's infinite wisdom gave me the power to make a choice. I fell asleep and had a dream.

In this dream, I was in my bed, and ghosts were flying all around me, pulling me up toward the ceiling in my bedroom. Above my bed, a big hole was in the ceiling, an opening to go through. The ghost pulled me toward it again and again. Confused, I didn't know what to do. I was getting closer... and closer. I had to make a decision: go through or not.

I soon realized *I had the power* to break away and stop this. I put my hands and feet on the ceiling to stop myself from going through the hole. The ghosts were all through and I was left on all fours.

Next, I woke up in my bed, paralyzed. On my back, I couldn't move my legs, arms, or body. Only my eyes could open; they moved from side to side. *I tried to move*, but I couldn't. In my amazement, I understood my dream. I had to lay quietly. I made a decision to stay alive, deal with *my problems,* and figure it out. It took me 10 minutes before I could move. God gave me a choice to live or die, and I took life!

9

I was seeing a counselor and told her of this dream. She said, "You were given a life or death choice, and if you went through the circle (hole in your ceiling), you would have died." It became so real to me, that I again knew He was not finished with my path. The paralyzing part was my body came back to life, with regained strength and purpose. So I used that power to make it through and I did! Thank You, Jesus!

The long, drawn out divorce happened, and I moved three hours away to another state. I reclaimed my life. I was just far enough away to be able to have connection with my oldest two children. He was working and she was finishing high school and going onto college. I thought I was in the clear, but the rock was thrown through the window again.

In 1995 (now three years after my divorce), I made the move. Five days in my new state and town, just settled in. My gynecologist, Dr. P., called about a checkup before I moved. She called me to share the results of my pap smear. I had just had a pap smear in May, this was September. Not sure I would find another doctor to my liking when I moved. In May 1995, all of my tests came back clean. September 1995 was just a precaution, and I'm glad I did it. This test came back with cancer!

Five months after I had a clean pap smear, I found out I had endometrial/cervical cancer, a fast growing one, and not a lot known about it. I was sent to the University of Pennsylvania hospital to a specialist, Dr. M., and got the worst news: I had 6 to 9 months to live and had to get my life in order in two weeks, as I was having surgery. Daughter #2 was 12 years old, in sixth grade. What do I do? I go to an attorney (a family friend) to get my will in order, and put a guardian in place for my 12 year old. I talked to my nurse, doctor, friends, and asked their opinion. I proceeded with my calendar of dates.

On October 27, 1995, I had a radical hysterectomy. Everything came out, then chemotherapy for six months. Daughter # 2... where will she go for a week as I am in the hospital? Schedule it over a long weekend so she doesn't miss a lot of school? Send her to her father's? He doesn't want her and his new wife is pissed, but she goes. She can see her sister and brother, and they can help her to adjust since no one really knew what to expect.

My surgery was set for laparoscopic; three cuts, belly-button, right, left, hip area. They take it out hoping for no complications. But to my surprise, there are. So I'm cut from belly button to crotch, straight line down. They check the type of cancer. They were afraid of not getting it all and leaving cells behind. One hundred staples later, three hours in surgery had turned into five on the table. I'm now in recovery and they woke me up, slapping my face and forcing me to be awake.

Finally I am awake somewhat, and they tell me there is a problem. I have to go back for more surgery. My blood test came back saying I am bleeding internally. I will be dead in 20 minutes, so off we go, running me down the hall on the table back into the OR. Adrenaline soaring through me, I am awake. I felt like one of the hospital shows on television! Everyone is scurrying, things dropping, noise beyond loud, yelling, 15 people around me, hooking me up to monitors. My arms stretched out like Jesus on the cross. I could only move my head. I knew I was going to die.

Becoming more awake, I started yelling, "Put me out!" The anesthesiologist was saying, "Relax." I yelled for my doctor, screaming his name. I yelled over and over. He came and I said, "Put me out now." They did and proceeded to open me up again and begin.

I remember being in recovery again. A nurse was talking to me, asking questions as they do. Trying to get me to focus and be awake. This was different. She kept saying daughter #2's name and asking me who this name belongs to. When I could fully focus, I answered it was my 12-year-old daughter, why? She said that all I kept saying was,

10

ENCOUNTER # 3

October 27, 1995

"Not now, Jesus, there is no one to take care of her', 'Not now, I can't go!'" This nurse said I kept saying this over and over again. So she wanted to know who I was protecting. To this day, it makes me cry, and I can't believe it happened. God saved me again.

To the answer of my three hour to five hour to seven hour surgery, nothing had happened. I wasn't bleeding internally; the nurse had just taken blood from the wrong arm, the one the intravenous was in, and the watered down blood came back with the wrong account. So the second surgery was not needed. I found this out the day after, when the doctor and anesthesiologist came in my room for the routine visit. I was horrified that this could happen in such a prestigious hospital in this country. Everyone said I should sue, but I had to sue the doctor and the hospital. My realization was, the doctor did as he thought was correct and saved my life. The hospital was in the wrong. I couldn't sue one without suing the other. I decided not to proceed with a lawsuit. I had my life and God saw to it that I would be okay. So was daughter #2.

My hospital stay was over and I was at a friend's house. It was time to call my ex and have him bring daughter #2 to my friend's house. I stayed for a few days to recoup. My ex was so angry and said, "I just should have died, to make everyone's life easier." So I recouped. In the next two months, I cut my hair very short and started chemotherapy. My first chemotherapy was December 13, 1995 at The University of Pennsylvania hospital. It was hard. I was so sick and had to go back and forth (a 2 ½ hour drive). When I got home, I was very sick for five days. I knew this wasn't going to work, because the travel time and conditions were too hectic.

I switched to my new area and found a great center to perform the rest of my chemotherapy. I needed to have this for the next six months. They were terrific! In five week's time (January 5, 1996) I lost all my hair and the plan for survival began. I went every three weeks for a five hour session of chemotherapy. I was down in bed for four days and was so sick. Vomiting, passing out, nauseous. The nausea drugs didn't help, but I kept trying. It was just daughter #2 and me. My date and I were estranged, had broken up, and I was on my own again. All to my benefit, and it built a better trust in my faith.

I was thankful that God saved me again. I had my children and my life. I'd met some really great people in my new town. I'd gotten involved in some activities. I finished with my chemotherapy in April 1996 and moved on. I visited my friends and children in the other state. I became very happy, always knowing I had my best friend, GOD, in my heart and also having my back!

This became a new path, a new challenge. It wasn't always comfortable, but it was manageable. The normal problems with a teenager came. My boy and girl #1 became their own. We all survived and moved on to our own greater place. It was a fun, sometimes hectic place, but it was home. We made it home. My other children came and visited. I thought I would move back to the other state then, but it didn't happen. I stayed where I was, knowing in my heart that you don't go backwards.

11

A few years later, I helped my son buy a house in the other state. Meanwhile, daughter #1 was in college, out of state. She wanted to move back, as well. So I got them all set up in their hometown, in the house at number 54, as we called it.

It was 1997 now and all seemed good. I met a guy in 1997 and we became friends and kept in touch. Nothing more at the time. I only wanted friends. My life was less complicated and everyone was thriving, moving on the path of life and happiness. My friend had been away for a while and came home in the spring of 1998 and we connected again. To our amazement, we realized we both wanted more, so we started dating. Shocked, we really hit it off well. He enjoyed my life and I his. Even daughter #2 at 15 years old enjoyed him. We laughed, did crazy things, and started to really have fun. Even boy and daughter #1 would visit and have a blast.

It was April 1998 while I was eating dinner when I got

a phone call. My ex was in the hospital (he was 46 years old) and it wasn't looking good. I needed to get to the other state and bring daughter #2. We packed up and went to number 54 house. When we arrived at the hospital, my ex's family were all there. One at a time, the children were let in to see their father. Then all three of them went together. I didn't want daughter #2 to be by herself. She was only 15 and scared. I was not allowed to be in the room, so in the waiting room, I stayed.

His new wife would not allow me to be in his room with my children. She wanted me to be thrown out of the hospital. A social worker was called in and said that wasn't going to happen, these three children need to be here with their mom, so I stayed, but out of the way. To this day, it still baffles me. What I learned, in time, was that my ex always talked about me. He was an alcoholic and drank much. We finally got to understand what happened.

I was finally allowed to see him, his new wife left to go home, get fresh, before she came back. I went into the room to see him, and I talked to him. He knew my voice; the nurses said his reaction was because of this. He threw his arms up in the air. The nurse said that was his first response—to my voice. He twitched and moved, and then I was asked to leave, as to not overdo him.

Trying to understand exactly what happened to him, the answer is a little hard to accept. Being an alcoholic for so many years had taken a toll on his body, as the doctors explained it. His esophagus burst, and he was bleeding out. The doctors said it is like a balloon: the blood circulates through the body, around the body back from the heart to the liver and back again. The liver cleanses the blood and sends it back to the heart and the rest of the body. The heart moves the blood after passing through the liver faster than the liver can process. There was a backup of blood into the liver and the esophagus vessel blew up. Much like a balloon would burst.

He was put into a drug-induced coma and stayed there for three weeks. Every time they tried to take him out, the DT's kicked in and they had to put him back under. After many weeks, he was able to come out of the coma and was transferred to a big hospital in New Jersey for a liver transplant. This came with a life altering change—not so sure he was going to manage that. Fifteen hours after being transferred, he had a massive heart attack. His body could not take the strain. I remember the 3am phone call from his sister alerting me. All she kept saying was, "He's dead, he's dead!"

It was a shame. All I could think about was my children. Daughter #2 and I were on our way up to the other state, so she could see him again that weekend. Now we had to go for my other two children and act accordingly. They were all so devastated, and to my surprise, it hit me harder than I thought it would. We had been together almost 25 years. Things fell apart. But God's great glory, He had ruled again. The timing was hard and it hurt all.

The viewing was huge, and all the people I hadn't seen in so many years were there. His wife wanted me thrown out of the funeral home. To my surprise, everyone took over, but I stayed in the back out of the way. Also surprised, everyone came to see me. The next day at the funeral/burial site/church, his wife wanted me thrown out. She said that I did not belong there. Again, to my surprise, the priest doing his service at the church said, "This is God's house, everyone is invited!" His wife of two years, and her mother, even tried grabbing my arms, just to throw me out! Again the priest said, "Stop." I stayed in the back of the church with one of the funeral directors. It was astonishing!

When we arrived at the burial, I waited in my son's car until all left. We didn't need anymore complications. My children came to get me, and I went to the grave. As they put the casket down, surreal is the only word I can come up with. My thought is and I always say, "God will only let you get away with so much. So be careful who you challenge and what you wish for." I believe this to my core and try to live it as best as I can. So as life does, and we do, we move on!

12

Many years have passed. It is now 2015 and life has been good to us. My son owns his own business and is doing well in the other state where he stayed. He is married with two children, one boy and one girl. We are not close. My love for him is eternal. Many things have happened. Too many to even talk about. He knows the reasons, and the ball lies with him.

Daughter #1 is also married and has two children, one boy and one girl. We have a great relationship. She also owns her own business and is doing well. She lives close to me. Not to say we haven't had our turmoil. We have fun and we love each other.

Daughter #2 is still single, lives about 20 miles away, and lives her own life. We go back and forth. One day on, one day off. I know we greatly love each other. In time, I can only hope love will out rule all.

Many changes and challenges, but *we are all we have,*

and we are still called *family*. Good, bad, indifferent, still family. And my soulmate and I are still together, going on 20 years. We're having fun and dealing with the perils of life and loving it. All just gives hope. So every day is something new.

13

It is now 2015 and I am on my way to see my gynecologist-oncologist, as I have done for the past 20 years, for my yearly checkup. I can tell by the way he is examining me (I have gotten to know now for a very long time), it's not good. He leans up against the wall and says, "I felt something, a lump." I say, "What? We need to get it out." He says, "Let's wait 'til next month and see," so we do. It got bigger and in August 18, 2015, surgery it is.

He tries a new robotic technique, but too much scar tissue is in the way. So cut again I am, hip to hip. (After I had a 1998 tummy tuck to get rid of my other scar that made me look like had 2 ass cracks, one in back and one in front.) The three hour surgery goes well, but the cancer comes back, the same cancer I had 20 years ago, endometrial cervical. A 2½ cm tumor has grown to 6 cm—tripled its size in 60 days. That is not supposed to happen. It is a very rare, but it happened again. My cancer came back and it had to come out.

My only thoughts are, "How do I survive this? Will this time kill me?" My mind is not playing good with me. "What happens next? Oh, my God, chemotherapy again. Will my relationship survive? Will it be hard on all again? Can I go through this again?" my thoughts are raging. I don't know what to think. It was so hard on everybody 20 years ago. I did not know my soulmate then, and he has no idea what he is in store for. Maybe I should just die. It has been so much time. I will only let my close family members know. It is private.

I tell daughter #1. We start crying, but okay, we will get through this. I tried to call daughter #2. She doesn't answer. She only likes to text. I send her an email, no response. Not sure if she is hiding from the pain or if she can't go through this again. It hurts because she was there 20 years ago. I had to let it go. She's on another path. To each his own. I don't tell my son. He is also on his own path. We don't speak. So between myself, my SO, soulmate, daughter #1, and my doctor, we get the job done. My SO hasn't left my side. Two days in the hospital, same day surgery did not work, and my breathing and heartbeat were too low to let me go home. And the pain. On pain pills I live again. Only good thing: I lost 10 pounds.

Dr. A. says he got it. He peeled it off and it fell apart in his hand. He is so confident; I'm not so sure. He sends it off to the lab, and again endometrial/cervical cancer, fast growing. I am feeling defeated and can't believe after 20 years it came back. My same cancer. You are supposed to be good to go after 20 years. Again, "Why me?" Then I think, "Why not me? What makes me so special?" So I accept that if it teaches lessons, then let's go with it. And I really hope it does. So after six weeks, I start radiation. Seven weeks of being zapped, five days a week, weekends off. Start again for 34 radiation treatments.

Thank God for the same cancer center I used 20 years ago. Different doctor for radiation. This doctor is a radiation expert, but still at the same place. Makes it easy. You drive yourself. It only takes about half an hour. This set up and a two minute zap. The staff is great—polite and encouraging. I'm not much of a talker of my private affairs. Everyone waiting there wants to tell their story: "What do you have?" So I stay quiet and to myself. I get through my seven weeks. Hooray, we can go to Key West to rest and heal! Soak up some sun and relax.

During my radiation five zaps in, I had a terrible sinus infection affecting my tooth that, 30 years ago, I'd had a root canal and capped. It has to come out, so to the dentist I go. And we pull the tooth. The pain is great, and the penicillin is prescribed; all is a go and healing. But when I am in Key West, I am feeling achy. I ignore it and take Zyrtec for allergies. It seems to help. Again, I am surviving the cancer and thinking it's all good...

14

ENCOUNTER # 4

January 2016
Re-Occurrence of cancer dream…

Two weeks before returning home, I get the phone call, its Dr. A., my gynecologist/surgeon calls. He says, "I have good news and bad news." My heart goes limp. My eyes fill and I have to sit down. He says that upon the panel review, plus all the pathology review 1995-2015, the group of 23 doctors feel it is in my best interest to have chemotherapy again. This is 2016. "Even though radiation should have done the trick, you did so well 20 years ago. The cells stayed at bay for 20 years. It is in your best interest to have chemotherapy again."

I start to cry and know it is for the best. To go through that again, lose my hair, be sick, puking, shots, all that goes with chemotherapy. I feel so defeated. It's my choice. Do I want this? Do I want to put myself through the agony and disgust I felt 20 years ago? In my heart, I know things have changed. Times are better, chemotherapy is supposed to be easier and not so invasive. How do I do this? My heart doesn't feel ready to go through this again. I'm scared, but I have to be hopeful. Back to the center, to my oncologist of 20 years ago, Dr. S., we go.

I am not feeling the best as we return from Key West, like I've got the flu. I'm feeling achy and ill. Four days down, no food, so I go for a pet scan. This scan makes sure there are no more lumps, masses, or other cancer. It has been six months since surgery. They are trying to see if any other tumors/cells have grown. I waited for my scheduled time and get the juice, and they radiate me through my body. All comes back good, except my sinus, that has flared up again. It never went away.

Off to get a CAT scan on my head for the sinus. The pain of the sinus is astonishing and debilitating and has me down and out! On medications and big pain pills again. The pain is so bad: it goes through my head, down my back into my hips, down my legs. I can't even describe the pain. It's just horrible, but I go to the ENT. Another Dr. S. and I am put on steroids, nasal spray. If it doesn't clear up, then I have to have sinus surgery. Chemotherapy will have to wait again, so on we go. I can't understand why this is happening. *I am beyond grief.* I just want this to be finished. But in God's great wisdom, He has a plan. Not my plan, but His plan. Great!

15

ENCOUNTER # 5

February 21, 2016

Again, as always with me. I go to my bed. S O, next to me: he laughs at me because my dreams are always so cryptic and many come true. I am asleep and I am dreaming, it starts. I was trying to get away from people (mostly men) trying to kill me. I had to climb up, up, up. I was using hook type "J" to pull me up; some were made of animal hooves or rabbit paws. Whatever type, grappling hooks, always a step up to grab, to hoist myself up, to get away. As soon as I got up, I found more people coming after me. So I found more J hooks to climb.

One man helped me by putting me on his shoulders and pushing me up. He was a big man, tall, broad shoulders, keeping everyone else away, not wanting to hurt me. It seemed every tier I got to, my efforts had to start again. At one point, I thought I was on a pirate ship and scurrying away, hurrying away from all these people. Another was a cha-cha type of store and I used rails around the ceiling to elude them. But always going up, up, up to the next level.

Finally, I got to the top and saw the hatch cover in the ceiling, like an opening to your attic. I tried to push up the panel, but it wouldn't budge. Scared, I kept pushing harder and harder. Then all of a sudden, I burst out laughing, saying, "God, you are funny," and ending the dream. I was still laughing as I woke myself up from the laughter. As I woke up, I had to get a pen and paper, writing these words....

"The door it won't open,
God said, 'NO!
Your time is not over,
Get up and go,
Finish your story,
I'll tell you when,
As you have always known.
I love you, my best friend.'"

These words came to me and I was laughing. I woke up knowing to write them down. Still laughing because of my dream! Knowing what it meant. Since it has not been my first to know it is not my time. God makes me laugh. He really is funny and always wants us to know this. He wants my book to be written about my experiences to let people know how this works for me. Not everyone is going to understand nor believe. I do and someone else will. So far, this is my fifth encounter.

16

Now finally after five weeks of waiting and healing, I get my CAT scan to see where I am with my sinus infection, and three days later, the results. I am clean, clear, and infection is all gone! It has been a long six weeks of steroids, pain meds, and nasal spray (how do people use that stuff?). A good end to a terrible infection. I have *never* felt so much pain. Worse than labor, cancer surgery, and any pain I have ever felt. It's the end and I will proceed with chemotherapy.

My consult is in three days. I find out just what I will have and go from there: how much chemo, what kind of poisons, how many treatments. It's been a long nine months and the end to a beginning is happening. Now it's just the start to heal me again. All this time, I know I am in God's hands and He is carrying me.

Another consult and questions are being asked and answered. Over an hour and a new person is in the mix. Male nurse practitioner, a nice guy, much information, my head is reeling. In my mind, a blur, you would think it doesn't happen. But the 20 year similar treatment begins, back remembering things I thought I forgot. Guess what, they are back. Am I scared? Yes and no. I know a lot of what's going to happen. I did that, am I doing that again. Is that the nerves part? My age, 20 years older. My body, how much can it take? Big poisons again.

Today's the day for my port. Minor or not, surgery is no picnic. Thank goodness the team, doctors, nurses, and I worked well. It's over; it's in and it hurts. I feel pressure in my neck like muscles pulling. I don't want to move my head. Yes, pain pills; they work. Heal fast. Tuesday is only 4 days away and chemotherapy starts. At times, it's overwhelming and all I do is break down and cry my eyes out. But I know I needed it and have to get over it and move on.

Start again. I just got an uplifting phone call. Thank You, Jesus. When I was still low, a good friend called. "I'll call her Ms. Amazing." She made me laugh and smile! Yup, just what God ordered! Feeling good, smiling, moving forward. It puts you back in sync. Please don't stop, it works, and much needed. Just what I needed, thank You, Jesus.

So off to speak to Dr. S. He says we will do 4 treatments, 8 sessions, instead of doing full sessions, we will do half. It's better for your body. Two weeks in a row, one day, and a week off. So you can rest. Then start again 2 on, 1 off, you will be able to accept this way a lot better. We will start next week and...

17

Today is my first treatment. I can see on my S O's face , concern, intrigue, help I need to know. He has never been through anything like this and he needs my help. I will have five bags of drugs. Bag number one is a cleaning solution, basically, that goes through my catheter through the needle, gets pushed in the port, and the drip starts, cleaning the port. The catheter into the vein into the artery. This is an important step that will take half an hour.

Bag number 2: nausea meds, Benadryl, steroids—a mix that will take half an hour. Will make me easy, loopy.

Bag number 3: Carboplatin chemotherapy. This takes 45 minutes. The drip is slow

Bag number 4: Taxotere chemotherapy. This is the toxic one. Takes about an hour. It's slow drip, at first, then add to the combination, using both the Carboplatin and Taxotere at the same time. The doctors have come up with this recipe for my treatments, to help me heal of this cancer. They told me that alone, each one would kill me; as a combo, it works, so we go to it.

Bag number 5: Finish the cleansing solution to clean all of the excess of any of the four bags and to give my port/veins to artery a cleaning. Takes about 45 minutes.

When the last beep on the intravenous machine goes off, I am done for the day. Five bags in 4½ hours. Now I wait eight days to get session B, to equal one full treatment. They have decided for my own benefit to give me half treatments two weeks in a row, rather than one full treatment and one day. They feel it is better for my body on half treatments, than a full one and knock me out completely. So I guess we will try this and see how it works. Truthfully, I'm feeling pretty good after 4½ hours of getting nothing but intravenous drugs. I know I can handle it and we keep moving forward.

18

Today's part B of treatment number one. Not sure how this will work. I'm here and we are starting, putting my Elmo cream on my port. Supposed to help with the pain when they stick my port with the needle.

So we start with bag one to cleanse the vein/artery (20 minutes). Go to bag 2 of mix drugs, Benadryl, steroids, nausea (about 30 minutes). Go to bag 3: carboplatin (45 minutes). Bag 4: Taxatere (about 45 minutes). Bag for cleanse. Finish bag number one (15 minutes).

Treatment number one is completely finished. Just a little over 2 hours this time. Wow, now that was not so bad. I really thought it would be longer. Out the door on my way. Next week is my off week. I'm feeling really good. Some nausea, tender tummy but again no vomiting. So glad they are doing half treatments. One down, three full treatments to go.

I am on my off week now and am doing really good. My tummy is still tender, but these half treatments are working. I am not vomiting. That is a relief. Twenty years ago, I was down 5 days after my treatments. A whole day process. This seems to be working with half treatments two weeks. A week off and then we start again. To me, this is much progress.

Today was my mid-week checkup, taking blood for blood work and checking up on my cell count. When I started, it was perfect. After my first half treatment, it went to 1.4. Now after a full treatment, I'm down slightly to 1.2, but that is okay. Monday, I go for the start of number two's treatment and, again, below 1.0 is a sign of needing Neulasta shots to keep cell counts in a good-to-okay level.

Today is Monday and I am getting juiced. My blood work was tested for levels first to make sure I can tolerate chemotherapy again. They are much higher, a 1.8, back up and a good sign. Juicing starts again, five bags routine: shots, cleanse, meds, carboplatin, taxotere, and cleanse. This time, only three hours since everything is going well. The drips have increased; they were able to run the drips quicker as I am tolerating a much faster flow. Yes, it makes you feel loopy, too. I'm the only one left in the clinic. Everyone else is finished for the day. Some come for an hour, others more, some less. But I'm alone here.

I sent my S O doing errands; no need for him to sit when he can get things accomplished. I love him to the world and back, but sitting here staring at me is unnerving! I know he looks at me like he's waiting for me to break. I also know that time is going to arrive: my hair is going to fall out. Starting to get clumps. I'm sure after this session, it will really start falling out. I only wish it will all fall out at one time as it did 20 years ago. I can tell you, it was easier to cope with. Please, God, allow me to do this again. Please, the tears come as I speak, but I beg You, please. I can take having a port, getting four full, 8/2 treatments, but losing my hair again just cuts me to the quick. I guess we all have a part of Sampson in us. I have a picture of me from 1995-1996 chemo days when I lost my hair. I will redo this picture again. A new picture, 2016, as a reminder is good and we need to know and remember being humbled, really humbled.

Treatment went well. I'm moving, feel loopy, and a little out of sorts (drunk like, but not puking). Thank You, God. I can handle tender tummy, that's an everyday event. The puking, it devours you and brings you to your knees. So again, thank You, God! Moving on, day by day. Next Monday is part B, then two full treatments done. Two down and two to go. Yay. Yay.

19

Today is treatment day again, number 2, part B. Same as last week. Feeling loopy and again out of sorts, wobbly, and a little bit shakier. Again, a little nauseous. That's starting to settle in what I call a little more than an upset tummy. Like I could puke, yuck. Tired, just want to not move and rest. I am relaxing and my tummy is getting worse. Really upset. Please let me sleep, take a nap. Cold, need a blanket. I remember this 20 years ago. This is how I felt every time I had treatments and I did puke, really puke. The more juice, the stronger the reaction, but I just keep moving forward and need to keep the results. The more treatment sessions, the colder I am getting, all the time feeling cold.

People are walking around me in shorts and t-shirts. I have on my UGG boots, pants, and a fleece and I am still cold! It's 85 outside. My cell counts were down a bit from 1.08 to 1.05. May not seem much, but my body can feel the difference. I'm much colder. Just put on another layer. On and off, whatever is needed.

And yes, my hair is falling out handfuls in the shower. All the dark color is on the shower drain and, I'm sure looking grayer by the minute. I cut it short, but I'm going to go shorter, buzz it. Maybe I'll try a little more wacky style before the rest of it falls out. It's less stress when real short hair falls out, than when it is in longer strands. I lost my hair 20 years ago and didn't think it would bother me as much this time, but I was wrong. Hair is a big part of life. Yes, it grows back, but bald is harmful to your psyche, at least mine. I know it will happen, but I don't have to like it.

20

My temper is a lot more short, curt, not much patience. For as much as people would love to understand, they don't, and they just can't. They haven't been through it. Anyone can't unless they have gone through this whole cancer battle. I know they are feeling my pain and want to help, but you can't take away my inner being of feelings. Thank you, but stop giving me what you would do because you can't really say what you would do! You are not here, in this land of cancer. You are not having poisons run through your veins, coursing through every part of your interior body. Please, I love you, but back off. Please stop your opinions. Your opinions, I love them normally. Not now, they really don't count, this is all me. It's all about me. You need to stop and understand.

I know it's hard, but please listen to what I am telling you. I can't handle it anymore. I am grumpy, and you are not helping. Please, I love you, but back off. I am and need to process this my own way, only my way. Please learn to accept me for now and love me back, hug me, hold me, stop acting like I'm a piece of china that's going to break. I am stronger than that. Maybe I just need your presence, not your mouth, tone, or anger that this is happening to my body, not yours. Get over yourself.

Stop looking at me, staring like any minute I will fall apart. Maybe I will, so what. I have learned to do this in quiet. In my shower is my crying time, not in front of you. You can't handle it. I want to scream, but I am private, and you can't handle it. I know you want to help, but please do as I asked, not what you think I need. I am the one who goes to their interior insider herself. Give me this time to think, to study, and to process. It is a lot and takes time, my time.

I know it may come off as hard for you, but action to a reaction on all sides. It's a common factor, and if I react, so do you. If you react, so do I. Common ground, as I told you from the start, I alerted you. Gave you all the facts. As I have done this before, I know how I will react. Please give me understanding, love, and peace; as least, please try... I love you always, yes.

I am calmer today, thank you. Now I'm on my off week. Wish I could rest more, feeling more fatigued. But it's all part of this play. I have rehearsed this before and now am praying all the parts fit together. Thank you, all of you, for your love.

21

Today is Wednesday. Time for treatment 3, part A. Half a liter of saline, meds, Carboplatin, Taxotere, finish saline, cleanse catheter port, and done. Today was only 2½ hours. We are really getting this down. Less time, bigger drips, runs faster. Yes, I feel like I'm drunk. Loopy, like waves are rolling in my head. Yes, nausea. It's stronger, but I'm also hungry. Going to get a vanilla milkshake. Yum, tastes good. Since I'm losing my taste buds, not a lot of foods really have flavor. In this treatment phase, it will get worse. I'll lose more. But it's all okay, I'll deal with it, that is the plan. Move forward and laugh, smile, and be strong. Thank you.

I realize this is mundane to everyone, but this is my life right now. The life of a cancer patient. Someone who is going through treatments and trying to have an understanding of that explained. So you may understand that it does get routine. That is that. We are in this routine and so want the outer cancer world to view this from us. We wish this were fun, but it's not. We wish no one ever has to have this routine, but people do and make the best of it. It's all anyone of us can do. That is why trying to have normal events every day through dilemmas (as regular happenings) is our goal.

As well, thank you for your understanding. You may not think it helps, but let me assure you, it does. You can't catch cancer from us. Cancer is not contagious. Please, when you see us around, smile, don't run. We are just human beings going through an ordeal just like all people around the world.

God has been a wonderful presence in my life, giving me comfort, calm, and much love. My inner being has held me. I do this as a best friend, a companion, and a confidant. You may think I'm out there, but I'm not. Just on focus to get the best for me to be able to handle my cancer, my way. With all the help I can get from all of my people, loved ones, friends, besties, and acquaintances, as well. Thank you all for your support. It is well needed and wanted. A very good friend of mine sent me this lovely poem, so I shall share with you:

"In case no one told you today,
you are beautiful, you are loved,
you are needed,
you're alive for a reason,
you are stronger than you think,
you are gonna get through this.
I'm glad you are alive,
and don't ever give up."

Thank you, my friend (Ms. Amazing) for this! It means more than words can ever express.

22

Today is after chemo day. Same routine, same timing. I'm done. I am exhausted. It's 5:30am and I am wide awake. I'm sure it has to do with the meds I've been given. There is a steroid treatment in the mix. Better to help; as they say, sleep is overrated. I'll catch some Z's later.

I noticed my eyebrows are thinning and my eyelashes, as well. Many have fallen out. Thinning body hair is not only related to a person's head, the whole body gets into the act! My project is to get a photo taken. The only photo I have is the old one, so I'm going to redo that photo again. *This is for me.* This is my way of remembrance. It's more like atonement, to be grounded, humbled, whatever the verbiage used. I looked at that photo every day in my prayer book as I read my thankful words. Prayer puts me back, it grounds me. I was getting ready to celebrate 20 years clean, a survivor. My celebration has to be in a different understanding today. It is, "I'm alive." Don't take it for granted! I have survived cancer **again**. And we start over. Every day is a great day.

I say thank You, God, for letting me awake with this sun. It's another day. I say thank You, God, for giving me today, it is nighttime and time for rest. I made it again today. I sleep to start anew in the morning. I have to keep thankful because the whole universe is God's way of giving us life, freedom, challenge, comfort. I forget that often, and sometimes I need a push to be reminded. I guess it's my way to understand God, His never wavering love for me. I always learned how to accept what I can't, but want to understand.

23

Just looking around my life. I have much love, human love, shelter, food, air, sun, trees, extras, a body that works, plans. I can write, read, express, explore, explode—all of this is human. Not to be taken for granted. We need to remember what we have; this is not a right that is only given. Just as we work hard to earn, we need to work hard to survive. No one owes us this life. We are here to do better, to help each other. We should understand our chapters in our own daily survival.

Think about it: freedom of choice, what a wonderful concept! Given to all humans. To all, yes, everyone. Go deep within yourselves and find yours. See how you were, tick, and do. Learn to love you, you're the best. No one can take that from you. Only if you let them. Don't give up on yourself. You are important. You are allowed to grow in maturity, to be you. Please go and be your best. It is for you, and if you want to share, pick those to share you with.

You have that freedom of choice. We learned this and God has told us this. So use it to your best ability. It has been bestowed on all of us.

24

This week has not been a good week. Feeling poorly. Fatigued, really tired, like I've been hit hard (I have) and don't want to eat. But know I have to. Nothing tastes good, nothing. Every part of me is crying, screaming, really pissed off.

Right now, I am feeling very alone. No one can get the feeling. My hair, eyebrows, eyelashes, all falling out. I just feel so ugly, ashamed, embarrassed that I am hiding. Yes, hiding. I'm in the house, my room, my own body. Who wants to see me, see anyone. I surely don't.

Some people are really concerned, and some aren't; they just want to know the inside scoop. Have to know! Well, you don't need to know my pain and my emotions. We are the cancer/chemo victims, the ones going through this pain. Yes, it is very painful. The heart wrenching pain. Show a good face on the outside, but it's hell on the interior. Even if you want to explain, no one understands how this takes you to a point of isolation. Every cancer victim feels this. Yes, I know, I'm on round number 2 and it sucks, so we grieve in quiet, keep our emotions to ourselves.

People try to understand; maybe they feel they have to. Maybe they feel they want to. But understand: unless you are in my shoes, you can't. This too is understandable, but sometimes annoying. Sometimes, we just need our own time to process and feel. Someone said to me, "You need to adjust." Well, guess what, YOU go adjust! Adjust? What do you think we are doing? We are having the biggest adjustments we can think about. Do you want to be in our shoes? Do you want to trade places with us? If you do, please step up. That means every part of our daily routine. You may take over.

We all have our trials, and we need to go through them. Some have more, some are harder, but *we all have them*. Accepting them is the hard part. Yes, God says "He will not give us more than we can handle." That's good, because I don't want to handle anymore! I just want to get through and be whole again. To be better and wholesome. To not feel confined and ugly. I thought this would not hurt so much, but I can tell you, it does. All the things you think of—will I live through it, it is my time, did I do all my arrangements, who do I ask for help, do my finale— everything that a brain can think of.

It is going to happen. Do I let it happen? Who's fighting for me? Along with me? Who's in my corner? My protector? My confidant? Who do I trust? Your mind is in a whirlwind. You just don't want to care, but you do. You have to. All these things you are not ready for but are planted in your mind. To take care of you. It sucks, but you have to get through because you know you are the best to handle you. Your needs. Your expectations. This is all about you. Please remember that. Always. As I've said before, God gives us a choice. So use it for your best you. You choose.

Thank you to all who understand, and to those who want to and may. Please hug that person today, every day. Show them what they are going through is important for them, and for you. Respect their journey, help them to make a difference and tell them, they matter. Many words heard. Just as many words said. Please, help heal with kind words and showing love through your powerful words. In many ways, we all need to show others. Give hugs, kisses, and smiles; as we all know someone out in this gigantic world Is in need of them today, tomorrow, forever.

25

Today is treatment 3, part B. As I said, part B was getting hard to handle. I was down and out for three days. Just not up to myself. Fatigue set in really fast and hard. Energy was nil, not a good sleep person in normal life, wanted so badly to nap, but I don't. Tired, and it only makes me feel worse. I dozed a few times thinking it was a half hour or more. I got 5 to 10 minutes, but at least I did.

Feeling loopy and my nausea meds in full swing. I have to eat and do. Had small amounts and doing okay. Made light dinner, salad and roasted vegetables; thank goodness, I love them. It's now 8:30pm and my stomach is not happy. My body is feeling depleted. It's 9 pm, I must go to bed. So I do.

By 10:15pm, I am up in the bathroom puking.This is what I remember 20 years ago. I was hoping to bypass this, but I guess the treatments gave me a reprieve and the full blown action is beginning. There is nothing I hate more than puking at any time. Get it over with and go to sleep. I'm so tired. My body won't let me sleep, and then there is the meds bag. Steroids cause insomnia.

It's 1am, so now I know my body is ready. I sleep for hours, thinking it is 6:00-6:30am. Guess what, it's 4:45am. Great, I'm wide awake. I lay there.

It's now 6am. I'm done, up and moving. Tummy showing signs of not being happy. So I drink liquids, a sip at a time. Try to calm the nagging tummy to relax. I hope you understand why I feel this is important to have you know and tried to give you the complete scene. It's not fun. It just isn't. I'm exhausted, but can't sleep. Hungry, but afraid to eat, not wanting to puke again. This is a normal day for my chemotherapy treatment. So deal with it is. Deal, as we all have to figure out the best way.

This has been my off week. Friday is blood work day. Hoping my counts will be up some or just enough to be okay. Turmoil week again: tummy ache, still not happy, eat very small amounts, less, just to get by. And on we go. Not doing much, having tender tummy. It's painful and makes you not want to do anything. Just not moving and be quiet. Like, don't touch. So I've lived on soup and grilled cheese; meats are not in my diet right now. Too heavy to handle, too much to digest. As what goes in only comes out. It's like a pipeline. To the start and finish. Never thought going to the bathroom could be so tiring. But this is it. So all, be thankful , that I still can, and on my own.

26

Today is Wednesday, treatment 4 part A. Today means this is the last of 4/8 cycles of chemotherapy treatment. I can't believe I have got finished with mine. I see it ahead of me. Thank You, God. Thank you, Jesus, for being my inner strength. Making me see beyond human condition. Helping me understand this journey has a beginning and an end. Loving me unconditionally. Humans just can't do that. Teaching me how to accept myself in any form. On days when I have felt ugly and on days when I have felt beautiful. On days I was in worldly strength and days when I was the weakest. Thank You.

At the clinic having the needle put in me for the umpteenth time. First blood work to check my status, cell counts. I know they are low just by the way I have been feeling the past few weeks. They are .07. Below 1.0 (the good range) that is the cutoff line. Dr. S. tells me danger zone for infection, so watch what I do, who I am in contact with, where I go. All could send me to the hospital, not a place I would prefer.

We start with bag one, saline which runs all the bags. The next is mixed meds, makes me loopy, putting me in la la land. It's okay, because I can laugh. Then Carboplatin (the killer), Taxotere (the other killer), and let the saline clean the port, veins, and arteries. They all work together to make me whole, kill the bad cells, and clean my body. It's about three hours. I'm loopy, tired, and weak, but I'm strong. My will is strong, not giving up on this portion. Cycle is done, so we're finished with my treatment, part A. Now for next week, for part B.

As a thank you, my S O goes out and gets lunch for the amazing staff of nurses. Our way to thank them for all of their kindness and knowledge, positive action to help. *We, the cancer victims, need these nurses*! We could not go through this without them. As well as the doctors. *Dr. S., thank you.*

Tomorrow, I have to come back and get my Neulasta shot, bring up my low cell count as I did 20 years ago. I had to have five shots equal to this one shot and this is the only time my counts have been below 1.0. Close, but thanks for that. Steroids kicking in as I am up wide awake at 5am. Writing all parts of this process.

Hair falling out, eyelashes, eyebrows. Not much hair left on the rest of my body, not that I am hairy anyway. Wonder what this time will be. How things will grow back. I really wish to be pure white haired classic age. Could care less if legs and pits grow. Never got pit hair back so I'll keep that one. Hate to shave anyway. This is really comical. Just have to have a hearty laugh. Thank You, God, more of that to come.

27

Today is Friday, two days after 4 A treatment. I can sure feel the difference. Things changing, surging through my body. Steroids kicking up energy. Good, but also bad; crashing is a downer. But I got a full night's sleep. Woke up at 6:30 am, so I'll take it.

Something new: my eyes are not focusing. They are acting like they are kaleidoscope eyes. Just keep twisting the tube of colors and the outer ring twists, too. It's an unnerving feeling trying to focus. So many colors. The rainbow is invading my peripheral vision. All the rainbow colors to my vision are making me feel vulnerable. My equilibrium and nauseous tummy almost feel like I will fall.

It's been hours now. Getting better, maybe a little breakfast needed to help sugar levels to write and focus. Vision coming back stronger. Eyes working, so this day may start. As the day has been progressing, my eyes are about 75%, so I'll take that and surge forward. Going to relax this weekend and prepare for my last treatment on Wednesday. Thank God for all the help in getting through this. Angels on my shoulders and many prayers. Thanks to you all.

28

Oh my gosh, I can't believe today has arrived. It is Wednesday, June 29, 2016. The day I received my last chemotherapy treatment! I have so many emotions, I'm having a very hard time with how to react—elated, scared, wonderful, contained, overwhelmed, panicked in all, strong.

Thank You, God, for bringing me to this day of importance. It's my day to celebrate freedom, success, winning, the start of a new beginning. The road is going to be long and hard, nervous, but every time I get a good report, my stats come back with negatives on them, the goal is one more day in survival. I have survived another bout with cancer. Not just cancer, but a death with cancer.

I am one of God's angels. He needs me and I so need Him. He has told me so many times throughout my life. As well as showing. Even when I felt I was not good enough, God did. He raised me up, held me to Him and said yes, as I said yes to Him. I have never forgotten that.

Made mistakes and a lot of errors. I knew He loved me, loves me. We have a bond no one can break. Again, thank You God. Sometimes I don't always understand, but in my heart, I do. So I try my best in the mission, journey. I travel with lots of help along my way. As I am getting my treatment, my wonderful nurses came to me and said, "Your counts are not really good, but the treatment will be given and tomorrow you need to come back to get the last shot to bring up your cell counts. This will help with infection. So be careful of who is in your space. No one with any illnesses, cough, etc." So I can do this. I will do this. I have to.

As I am going on in life, I can finally say, I am finished with my chemotherapy treatments. I went through four cycles, eight treatments, each half at a time. Two Wednesdays on, one Wednesday off. It is a three week a month process. You start again. I was juiced for a time of three months, April through June 2016. I am free to go back to my everyday life. This will really be celebrating July 4th, 2016. Doesn't mean I stop everything now. I start my survival mode. I have my checkups every three months, get my CA 125 blood work and whatever else they wish checked, and every day, pray for great results.

It's the 4th of July and my body tanked, energy level tanked, don't want to eat, just feel drained. But this is normal when you have cancer treatments. The harder your body needs to fight, it's doing the job killing the bad cells, but also killing the good ones. A poison can't be put in and not take out the good as well as the bad. It's just as if you didn't change the oil in your car, just added more oil to the dirty oil. Dirty would overtake the good and would have to keep adding more or change it all together.

The more chemotherapy treatments are a good thing; that's why they spread them out over a period of time. Too much, too fast—bad results. Hospital stays are not what we are looking for. Keeping our bodies well and able to cope is the result. Slow and steady wins. As it goes, things have to go down before they go up. Keep to fight on and push forward. Keeps the momentum level. We as cancer victims know how to make our body shine. The lesson is teaching those who do not know how to help us fight this battle.

I may be finished as treatment goes. As you fly, you give yourself time to get back in sync with everyday life, to power up, eat, move, breathe, become your original self. The same with us, the cancer survivors. Every day is one day closer to winning back our life. When you see someone who has been through the battle of cancer—they have lost their hair, eyebrows, eyelashes, skin may be pale—smile at them, treat them as a normal human being. Don't step away. You can't catch cancer. They want your support—not questions, not disdain, not review.

29

During this process of healing from cancer / chemotherapy / radiation, and all the factors that go with this trial, still other obstacles occur. I had just gotten my CAT scan after drinking 1½ bottles of contrast, having more of the intravenous contrast injected through my port. The scan starts. Only took minutes in the tunnel scanner. I am having chest, abdomen, pelvic area scanned. Finished this test. It's over, and I went out. Be on my way, doing my errands, all this time thinking (as I have had the CAT scans before), "That was easy, no complications." Got my errands completed and brought some sushi home for myself and my S O, to have a great lunch.

As I arrive home and approach my kitchen, my S O says, "Dr. S. called. You must call him." I looked at him and said, "This isn't good." I call and they say, "You must get to the hospital to the ER now!" I asked, "What's wrong?" They say, "You have a blood clot in your right lung. Please come to the hospital immediately." So I put my groceries away, look at my S O, and say, "We have to go now. It's a blood clot in my right lung." Not good.

So we go and get to the ER in about 20 minutes. They check me in and take me to a room and we proceed. This is about 1pm. No lunch. They do all the pre-checks, you wait, checks again, wait, get the CAT scan reports, wait. Call daughter #1; she arrives at the hospital. I sent S O home (he had a project he had to stop, that needed his attention). We are waiting for answers to finally be told.

The clot is small. They feel not much to worry about, but needs to be addressed. If you have one clot in a lung, the chances are you have another clot in your legs. Who knew? I did not know this and they are going to ultra-sound both of my legs. I told them my ankles have been swollen for the past 2 weeks. I had taken a picture. I showed them, so the doctors could see how they look at night. We proceed with the test; the result is they are there. There is a bigger clot in the right leg, but also in the left. The test proceeds and they scan me right to left from hip to toes and she finds a clot behind my right knee. Not just a clot, but a 4 inch clot. Four inches, are you kidding me? Onto the left leg, and again behind the left knee, same as right, only a 1 inch clot. Behind both knees, then to the heart. Echo scanner comes in and does an echo scan of my heart. Nothing, thank God, but oh boy, does that hurt! All clear.

So now we go back to my legs. What do we do? They say sorry, but we are keeping you for the night. Need to monitor for 24 hours. I say great. It's 5:30pm and I'm starv-ing. Haven't have food all day. Daughter #1 and I wait for admitting to get my room ready. Daughter #1's husband G brings us dinner. Yes, thank you, G! As we are eating, it's time to move to my room. Will call my S O, give him all the news, ask if he's done with this project. Yes, he will be on his way to take over for daughter #1. I'm checked in, and all I want to do is go home. My answer to the clot is Lovenox shots (had them after surgery in August 2015 to stop clots from forming).

My night in the hospital was chaotic. I made it through and was released by 4pm the next day. I am home and need to go to bed, haven't slept in 24 hours! So sleep time now! Tomorrow is Dr. S. day and get all the info to get clots under control. Shots of Lovenox, two times a day. In my belly, yuck. For 30 days, 60 shots! Really?!

Then Dr. S. says, "Has anyone talked to you about your left kidney?" My S O and I look at each other and say "No!" Dr. S. says, "Okay, you have a lesion, cyst on your kidney. Usually, they are water, but yours is not." Again I say, "Really?!" I ask, "What do we do?" He's going to check my pet scan and CAT scan, and compare my new CAT scan to see where we are. Again, I say, "Really?!" So we wait!

You think you are home free, mending, and slam... black and blue from shots, nowhere to go, spaces all covered in purple. And they F'ing hurt. Another hoop to jump through. So we are waiting, day after day, shot after shot, my belly is so stung, for a good 20 minutes. Can't sit, stand, or walk. Dammit! Come on! Enough! Also all through this, my hair is still falling out, my eyelashes are gone, my eyebrows, gone! Paint those babies in when I need to look presentable. All I can say is yuck, yuck, yuck! But I also know I will get through. I always do!

30

It's been almost 30 days, 60 shots, and three to go and I am finished! Yay! Had my CAT scan, my vascular scans, ultrasounds, legs, chest, kidney. Now it's Friday. And we go get the results. Go see Dr. S.

Clots, left leg, gone! Yay, right leg, better, pills to work on those clots. Six months on Xarelto. Right lung, gone! Yay! Progress... Kidney, no change, but it's not cancer. Wow, thank God! Cyst, so I become the watcher, hoping everything goes away. They can remove my port. Happy day! This is all good news. I can see in Dr. S.'s face he is smiling, so he makes us smile. He's happy, giddy, almost upbeat.

He says, "This is all great news. You are CANCER FREE! I don't have to see you until October." I get six weeks to be a normal human. I feel like I can breathe. Deep breaths. Wow! It finally happened! God's light has sent me my sunshine, my rainbow, my life! Thank You, Jesus!

Now that a year has gone by from 2015-2016, I get to start having plans. I get to start making plans. I can begin to try to be normal, spur of the moment. Be spontaneous, make plans on when! You don't know how wonderful that feels. Just to be me. Just to be me! Tears are running down my face and air is gasping in my chest.

My heart is overwhelmed, almost palpitating. Look at my body; it has been cut, bruised, shaved, prodded, black and blue, loss of hair, all, any hair, swollen, dehydrated, fat, skinny, bloated, ugly, beautiful, scared, elated, nervous, angry, pissed off, happy. And now, it's over, just now, all over. Now all I can think to do is smile, just smile! Say thank you, my prayers have been answered. Now it's time to do the work of living. Yes, to God. I will live!

PART II

31

ENCOUNTER # 6

October 16, 2016
Eulogy/ Obituary Dream

G od told me in my dream, " I must write my Eulogy, my Obituary. So I got up and wrote it. It was not easy. Knowing I was not dying, I had to write it down with this poem.

"Come to me with open arms,
My arms will always be there,
Come to me and hold me tight,
My arms will never fail."

32

When I encountered the number 4 dream, I knew every minute *I had* to start writing this book. Not knowing where to start, or how to put the chapters together, or what words need to be printed, I just began using this pen, this journal, and writing. As I have been engaged with God in this endeavor, He has brought me to many thoughts, realities, and words, so I say, "Thank You, God."

To my amazement, starting as a child, I always knew God was powerful in my life. I loved looking up at the sky to the sun. The cloud shapes and the blue were mesmerizing. Of course, the warmth of the sun. I guess that's when yellow became my favorite color. You can see so much in the sun. You get heat and light, and you get sunburned. You get power. Yes, the sun has always given me that feeling of power. Day is bright, to be able to do what needs to be done. Then she goes, allowing us all to go to sleep.

Rest our bodies. Awaiting her next arrival, giving us the power, strength, and ability to start again.

Day after day, year after year, and so on. Thank you, Sun! To me, how could anything be any better? I feel I use this to help me in becoming me. A child moves along finding the way, learning the concepts of human life and trying to put a personal puzzle together. Wow, are those pieces complicated! By all accounts, piece by piece, they fit and make this shape called you. In God's great plan, it works. Many times, I have said, "Okay, I can do this," and many times, I have said, "I can't," knowing deep in my heart I would.

We all have our personal journey to create and follow. That's what we give up, our "freedom to choose." God giving us free will. Some days where I thought I failed come to mind. The reality is, there's no failure. You just didn't finish what you started. If you think about it, that is correct. Our bodies are not equipped to do it all at once. Time is the healer, the thought process, the comprehension. As we grow, we learn, we absorb, we teach, we get better. We also forget to give ourselves credit for this understanding. It takes years, some more than others. We can't do it all in a flash (boy, that would have been great). So we work to our own power, grow our brains, watch our bodies form, and become whole. A wonderful human being. Knowing how great the difference is between every single one of us. Yes, we need to be personal. It is our God-given destiny. He created us for that reason. Personal. So I must say again, thank You, God.

God wants us to understand HIM, as well. He is the universe, the all-encompassing, and has given human form to be allowed to live, breathe, consume His expanse. Sharing with us His divine, awesome strength. He wants us to prosper, grow, and become whole. WE put the boundaries in our way. We cut ourselves off. We forget to finish what we start. Trying is also success. Finishing is just plain happy. Have you ever said, "I can't believe I did that?" I'm sure we all have. Good or bad, as we thought we have. Or, "I wish I hadn't said or done that." I can't take it back. But you are wrong, you can. Changing the course of your action is a way to take back. Most of all, as we forget and forget to use our morals, values, and manners, we get to say: thank you, I'm sorry, Can I help?, and I love you.

Selfish has become a staple in life today. *Mine* is an overused word, instead of share. Where did we forget to incorporate them in our daily routines? Parents are so afraid to say "NO" to their children today. They want to be their friend. UMMMM NO, you are the parent. There is enough time as you all become more adult to be both parent and friend. Your job as a parent is to teach your child. You so wanted them in your life. Their personality will come on its own. *By them for them.*

Parents need to help. We all make mistakes, but we do the best we can from our own experiences. The mold is cast for us to shape. Our children will reshape on the way to becoming them. Their own personal being. How great is that! Everyone has done it before us, and it's not going to stop anytime soon. Be proud of yourself and them. Disappointed? Sure, but the bottom line is to be proud. God has told us He is proud of us. Now it's our turn to say, WE are proud, happy, loved.

33

C ancer.
There's a sad reality when people ask, "How do
you feel?" You can only tell them. It sounds like you are
complaining, but you're not, you're explaining the truth of
what is really happening. This is your life on a daily basis,
the whole truth of what you're going through every day.
No one can really understand, you know that.

Is everyone, even though they are asking, only asking
to be nice? Deep down, they really don't want to know. By
no fault of their own, they can't feel your daily fight, your
pain, your anguish. You want them to care, and they do.
They get tired of hearing the same words week after week,
day after day.

We, the cancer victims, understand, but we need your
support, love, and tenderness. We know it's hard on all of
us, but getting through every day is a struggle for us, as
well. Be patient, be kind, be helpful, because no one is

immune. Cancer can happen to any of us, at any time. No one knows when, where, or why, but we can only hope we are the last to go through this illness. Hope for the best!

34

Wow, it is now January 2017! It's been a long 2016. It's out, over. I can't wait for 2017 to begin. All my anxiety and fear to be left in 2016, but I have not been feeling well in my gut. I know myself; I want to push this away, ignore it, the feeling deep within me. I know I can't, but I sure am trying. I gave it September through December for my inner body. "You're fine," I have been told. "Smooth as silk, your cancer is gone. You're healing beautifully, smooth." But I don't get the numb, burning feeling coming through my left lower hip pelvic area. "Oh, it's nerve endings, could be from radiation. Give it a chance, you are still healing." My brain and my core are saying something different. I know in my heart there is a problem.

We are back home in Maryland. I know Dr. A. is coming Friday to our area. I'm going, I'm just gonna walk in. I need to see him. I decide and I go. Tell the nurses, Ms. N. Can I see Dr. A.? She says, "Sure, what's wrong?" I tell her, "Something is not right. I'm hurting, burning, and starting to have pain in my rectal area." I wait my turn and I am called in to the exam room. Dr. A. comes in, says, "Hello, what's wrong?" I explained my feelings and he checked me. Gives me an internal and feels something. Dr. A says, "Okay, need an MRI to define the cause." I take care of making the appointment three weeks later. An MRI shows a mass, tumor, about 1½ inches, so I go see Dr. A. And I'm in pain.

My rectum is bleeding, shooting pain, and I'm nervous. My fears are at a thousand percent. I see Dr. S., my oncologist, as well. His results are the same, tumor. So my team starts again. Next step is colonoscopy, a new doctor (Dr. R). I soon finished seeing Dr. A. I go to see Dr. R. Within 24 hours, I am asleep having a colonoscopy. I guess you could say it was an emergency. I go in and they put me to sleep, do the colonoscopy.

I wake up, find out now the pains in my rectum are from my prior radiation in September through early November 2015. I am burned internally and it's healing, not uncommon, nothing to alarm. Okay, I understand and handle this. Next, there is a tumor. It has not invaded my rectum, so we moved to the next step. Dr. R. took some biopsies and now we wait two weeks for the results. Dr. R., Dr. A., Dr. S., all have copies of my colonoscopy and now we wait the results. But I'm okay, knowing we have some answers is a blessing. I can at least accept the reason for this rectal pain and become the person to understand what's happening to my intestines. Knowing your healing, knowing your body, knowing your brain can make sense of all this.

Now to the tumor. When results come back and answers are given, a person can calm and come to a point of reason instead of panic. So we wait.

Well, it's three days later, in time for panic. It is cancer, round #3, the same cancer as in 1995, 2015, and now five months later after the all clear, after radiation, after 2016 chemotherapy, it's back. More tests and more results. It's not okay, it's not just healing; it's full-blown cancer again in my pelvic and rectum. Yes, it has invaded my rectum.

35

It's back, like a bullet. Invading my rectum, my ass! Oh, what do we do? Surgery, we are doing this again. I have to stop this cancer from spreading. This is February 27, 2017. I see Dr. A. Then Dr. R. Colonoscopy, the next day. He schedules me for my colonoscopy. As I said before, the same cancer, endometrial /cervical, I'm right back where I started 1995, 2015, and now yet again in 2017.

I know this is not good—all my pain, bleeding, and some healing. Most of all this damned cancer, so we start the process again. Life on hold. Cancer is number one. Has to be dealt with again. Has to be taken care of again. For vacation, we were supposed to leave (March 17, 2017) to go to St. Maarten. We also talked about going to St. Maarten in three weeks. It's paid for, and it's our yearly vacation trip. Oh, my goodness, I have really messed things up. Cancer again is ruling my life. We talk to Dr. A.. He says, "It's only a few weeks, maybe you should go, relax, calm down. It's planned, paid for, and scheduled."

They feel for my own psyche that I should go and have a good time. It's not till March 18, 2017.

Since my doctor, Dr. A, is going to be in my area on March 17th, I decided to make an appointment with him. If we do go on the 18th, I will be all checked out and feel more secure taking this trip. I go to see Dr. S. two days before that and I ask him his opinion. His opinion is, "This is cancer again. *You've just been through this.* You know the results and you know what could happen. I think you should skip the trip and have the cancer taken care of."

Okay, that's one great opinion, and he may be right. Now seeing Dr. A. Getting another internal, to be sure before we fly out the next day. Well, here we go! Dr. A. checks me, and it's not good. The cancer has grown, and it's spread down into my rectum. We all know what the answer is going to be. We cancel our vacation and set up for my surgery as quickly as we can. Sooner is better. Quick as Dr. A. can get it done.

My surgery is scheduled for March 27, 2017. One week to prepare, get my things in order, get my family notified, get ready for another cancer surgery. All of us are nervous. We don't know what we are going to find once we open me up. But hurry, we do. My life is in jeopardy, and cutting me open is the only way to know how bad this will be. I have one week to prepare. My cancer grew in eighteen days. Eighteen days on emergency alert.

36

I'm nervous, my body a wreck. This weekend (before) was exhausting. I stop all my vitamins. It's Sunday. I stopped the blood thinners. Saturday, my last food, I start my bowel prep: empty stomach, body, nerves. Monday morning (9am at Sinai hospital), I have an EKG, blood work, type and screen, and 12pm surgery. Oh, that agonizing ride to the hospital. Monday morning traffic, nervous, scared. Here we go again. All goes well. My S O and I get up to the same day surgery spot. He goes in the waiting area. I go into my pre-surgery room and get prepped. Now is the time to let S O in to see me. Daughter #2 is with him. They come to see me, give me kisses, hugs. Wish me and Dr. A. good luck and say I love you. I am on my way to surgery.

It's now 11pm and they are trying to keep me awake. My breath is laboring slowly. "Take a deep breath, Bonnie!" I finally get it and realize that I am in recovery. I ask what time it is, and they tell me 11pm. My surgery took longer than they thought, and I have been in recovery for over six hours. I am finally fine, so they take me to my room. The transport who is taking me is hitting every bump. I am moaning; I can't believe this is happening. We finally reach my room—my S O, daughter #2, and I. The nurses are in and out constantly. There is no relaxing tonight. Thanks for the drugs, so I can sleep.

The next day, I wake up sore. I asked what happened. I learned I was cut down my front, 18 inches, from under my boobs, to my crotch. Really, they tell me, the rectal cancer margins. Since I had extra intestine, Dr. A. could cut and put me back together. (I knew God did this).

We have a positive. I have a colostomy on my left side just under my ribs. Three to four months, then put me back together again. Dr. A. is positive we can do this. Now to go through what happened in the last 24 hours.

1. Got the cancer in my pelvis with good margins...*Check*
2. Got cancer in my rectum, cut out all tissue with good margins, saved my anus. "I have an ass..." *Check*
3. Looked at my scar, 18 inches from breastplate to crotch. Learning why, I say to nurse, "Now I have two asses again." Great... *Check*
4. Checked all my organs for signs of cancer. I have liver cancer... *Check*
5. Found three to four polyps on my liver, cut one off, cut in half, 1/2 to pathology, 1/2 for tissue chemo... *Check*

6. Loss of 1500cc of blood, received three units of blood... *Check*
7. Long surgery, five hours... *Check*
8. Long recovery, six hours... *Check*

As I remember talking in recovery, S O and daughter #2 were talking to me. I remember them saying, "Come on Mom, Bonnie, breathe!" And then I remember the people in the next cubby complaining as they were asked to leave their loved one. "Why do they get to stay?" Really, people, everyone is different. As S O told me, "It took *so long* for them to let them in, they gave them more time."

They told me that Dr. A. came and got them during surgery. He took them to another room to chat and give them the results. Dr. A. didn't want to talk in front of me as he didn't want me hearing about my liver, getting excited and overwhelmed. I'm okay with that (Dr. A. knows me) since we have been together for over 20 years. I want to know everything, but the correct time is the key.

It's the morning after surgery and Dr. A. comes into the room. Twenty-four hours later and he is with his P.A. (as I called them, his army). They checked me and we talk and they go on their way.

Hospitals are necessary; we need them. As to getting well, you have no time to heal! You get *no rest*; treatment yes, but the rest, forget it. I understand it, it's just the way it is. Yes, thank God for all of the nursing staff and doctors! Sleep, I could not find. To get out and get home was my agenda. I was there a total of four days. I worked very hard to walk, breathe, move, grow, strengthen, etc. to be able to go home. Get out of bed and move. I know for me this was my goal. On March 30, 2017, I was released late afternoon! All were very happy with my progress and we drove home.

The day before I left the hospital, my doctor said I could not leave without an MRI, so at 10:30pm, I was taken for a two hour MRI. I had never had an MRI for so long! Thank God the nurses were in tune with the time. They gave me my pain meds and some nausea meds. I could hardly stand to be in the tube that long. I fell asleep on and off, was relaxed, breathed, and got through. The only thing I asked them, "Next time, don't tell me the length of time left! When I heard only 20 minutes more, my body got anxious and wanted out." I almost squeezed the bulb (for out), but prayed instead. God, again, held me and got me through. By the time the MRI was over and I looked at the clock in my room, it was 1:30am. I couldn't believe three hours had passed. All I wanted to do was sleep. The night passed, the nurses came, duties of care were taken, every hour something to be checked.

Again, my goal was to go home, and I did in the morning. I was told, "Today, you go." Yes, I did it. Then we all were happy with my progress. Well, enough to leave, be released. My S O was getting the car and we were on our way home...

By the way, I need to tell you how wonderful it was to have him, my S O, with me from start to home. He stayed with me 100%, did not leave my side, slept in a chair, ate minimal, sought to meet my every need. He didn't leave me alone! I know God put him with me, my earthly savior, God's hand. Whatever you want to say. My human love.

Thank you so much, my S O, for loving me and staying by my side.

Also, daughter #2, she too was at my side, came every day, brought food, coffee, strength, and love, stayed late and took some burden off S O/me with her help, knowledge, compassion, thinking. She was and is a God send. Thank you, I love you.

Daughter #1 had been ill just before this hospital surgery. So her job was to get well, stay home, care for her family. My support was through her voice, which I also very much needed, so I thank you, love you, very much, my daughter.

37

Now we have arrived home. It was a long ride. Roads are not comfortable for the healing. Every time you think you missed one bump, you hit another. But home we are. It's Thursday, and I will sleep in my own bed. Yes, the next few days are good. Sleep, walk, sleep, move, sleep, rest. That is my routine. I haven't eaten much so I need to build strength. A clear liquid diet was my hospital stay. Food now was a war. My body didn't want anything. No chunks. We did smoothies, but after a few, I was done. We did things I wanted to, much too fast, my tender stomach yelling NO. I couldn't and would. No vomiting. So back to simple food and moving slow. I lost 10 pounds—not much, but the food was not my friend. Food is my power. I have to be able to try.

A lot was on my mind, I have this new attachment: a colostomy bag. I'm not accustomed to it and I'm freaking out about it. I feel grateful I'm alive, I can breathe, but I have a stoma that works as my anus. It is just under my left ribs. Your mind, body, and psyche all work to get you to adjust and I'm grossed out. Poop pass-through. I don't want to see this, it's gross, don't want to see poo pass-through! I don't want to accept this is my life for the next three months. So my battle begins. The battle of the wills.

I know I'm lucky. I will get mine reversed. I am not at the stable part of saying, "Okay, you got this. There is so much more in this new life." To all the people with permanent colostomy: I praise you all. You are so strong, brave, and soldiers, I commend you and thank you for your courage and strength.

It's a new lesson I have been taught. It has taken me several days to accept this new style of life, getting in the shower, standing nude, letting my S O and my daughter #2 bathe me, clean my poop, change my colostomy bag, putting it back together on my body. I'm not there yet to do it on my own. Thank God for the two of you, my family to help me. My anxiety goes through the roof when it is time to change and clean my new anus, called a stoma. As I say every day, "I have the day; I can breathe, move, I am alive. God granted me this so I must make the best. YOU can work with it." So work I will: eat more, get stronger, accept this challenge. Because you are alive, you can breathe, smile, love, embrace life. You are not alone. You have family, friends, and loved ones. You have your S O, who has never left your side. *Remember these are gifts.* Be grateful. This is what God has granted you.

38

It's now two weeks out of surgery. I'm much better, stronger. I've learned how to clean my colostomy bag. (Just think of all three children, the children you have brought into this world, the time you cleaned their butts —a mother 's job.)

Frightened, I'm still doing, I am. We can train our brains to do everything and now that's my goal. God gave me life, again. I want to use it to the best I can. I must accept this. Doesn't mean I have to like it. I tell myself that many times a day as I am moving forward. Only by this— my faith in God and my love for God—can I move forward. He is granting me this time to be alive and be thankful for. I am a blessing! I am a gift! I can breathe! I am God 's angel!

39

Today was my two week checkup with Dr. A. We both hugged each other when we saw each other. I thanked him for keeping me alive. He says, "Everything looks good, looks really good. So good. Your scar is healing 'pretty.'" Thankfully, no problems. All on course. They took the crossbar out of my stoma. All healing pretty. Working and functioning, doing its job. Okay, now to the good part!

What is our plan? Dr. A. is still wanting to start Cyber-Knife radiation on my pelvic and bowel area. Nurse N., after board reviews, thinks my liver needs to be a major focus, "As you can't live without a liver." I get that, too. I say, "All is good, but why can't we do both? Don't know which is going to go first. I don't want my liver to get lost, to be put on the back burner." As we wait for CyberKnife, Nurse N. says she'll have Dr. A. call Dr. S. (my oncologist) and talk to him, get the ball rolling on "CARIS" treatment, or something in the meantime to get started...

My fear: "CARIS" is genetically made DNA chemo to fit my type of clear cell cancer. My cancer originally in 1995 was endometrial /cervical; it's now being called a clear cell. It's still all the same cancer, just a more technical name. I'm on everyone's radar, but the timing is the key. Waiting for all the red tape to go through the process: to get the formula, to a finished product to get the chemotherapy that I need, delivered timing, and injections of the drug.

By mouth, a pill, intravenous injection, port are all factors to be planned. Dr. S. is the planner of that, so we are all on pins and needles to get this moving forward—sooner rather than later! I feel the same. Now please, let's get this started so we can punch this cancer to half time as a factor.

In my way, I have turned to God. God's power is the biggest, best power of all. He is my miracle. He says, "Now," so my words to heaven are, "Now, my Lord. Get them started now. Don't let them wait. Make them begin Your process in my healing to be healed. To be well, to be alive. In Jesus' name, Amen."

40

Today is Friday. Not only Friday, but Good Friday 2017. A holy day for many, as I am one. Today is a day of blessings and all who shall receive. Thank You, Jesus...

Today, I go see a new doctor. I will call him Dr. A. number two. He is a radiation specialist. He has been given my records and is a colleague of Dr. A. I was told he was very interested in my case. I'm excited, anxious, nervous. It's a 2 hour drive and my body (two weeks out of surgery) doesn't enjoy car rides. But, we are on the way, across the bridge to the western shore. My heart is racing as S O and I arrive.

Into the office by 8am and it's my turn. We go through all the mountains of paperwork, gave more extensive information, and wait for Dr. A. number two to come in. He is a gentle man, very soft-spoken, intrigued that I have all my dates and radiations. Question after question, we move forward in the information. He checks my scar, my heart, my body. It's about 45 minutes. He has me stand (as I get pain when I sit too long).

He says, "Let's get started." (I thought he was going to say goodbye!) To my shock, I'm standing and say, "Okay." He says, "Let's get a CAT scan, block your body, see where you are on the table. We may need to tattoo your hip and belly area." I guess I look surprised! He said, "You are here, there is no need for you to come back. Next week, we will call to start your treatments, the CyberKnife. It is radiation treatments with a robot pulsing through your body. Takes up to two hours to give and you must remain still." "What can you give to calm/relax me?" I ask. We finish this process and we leave. He says, "We will call you."

Today is Wednesday and I got a call from Dr. A. (#2). I AM NOT a candidate for CyberKnife. Disappointing, but I understand. Dr. A. called also to explain. I had a lot of radiation in 2015 by Dr. M. (thirty-four sessions), and with my body in its condition now (bowel cut out/put back together, healing, wanting to not have the colostomy bag after three months), Dr. A. said CyberKnife would destroy my rectum further and possibly my bladder and my kidneys. I would not be able to be put back together again. I'd lose my organ we have worked so hard to save. I cannot give up the job Dr. A. did to save my organ, my rectum. We work so hard to make me whole. So I shall be. I know it is in God's hands; He uses these wonderful men.

Doctors provide knowledge, fix organs, and give advice. At the end of the day, God's plan is powerful and I lean on His answers for my life. We now go to Dr. S. for chemotherapy and it's okay. I knew I would have chemo, as well, so now we fight this battle of chemo again. Thank You, God, for having other options available. I don't feel discouraged. I feel my life is saved. So we move forward on the next path. It is okay. I know God has my back.

41

This week is the never ending journey. I keep myself close to home, heal, have good days and bad. I try to smile because I only have my life to get me through. It's every day. You can either smile, cry, or give up. I choose to move forward, keeping my faith and believing God is my strength.

May 2 is port day. It gets put back in. I'm hating it, but I also know it's part of cancer. As they say, "You don't have to like it, but you have to accept it." Cancer sure does make you look at life with different eyes. You blink and change happens.

May 4, Thursday. I start chemo. Aggressive we will be. This must work (it's round number three). This hurts my heart. I know my body is tired, I know I'm doing my best. I also know this cancer could kill me. I know I also don't want this cancer anymore. Life is so precious, we forget that. It makes me think twice and twice again. No one knows what's in my body, they can"t It's hard to explain.

It's frustrating and angry. I know people try, but they don't live in me.

They think they have me, but do they? It may sound selfish, but it's not. May you never have to feel this and go through this. Help me, I need you. But try to understand: I am living this, me.

42

This week, I've been on the edge of my seat. This week, my port gets put in on Monday and chemo starts Thursday.

Monday: port day. All goes well, a different doctor (Dr. C.), is doing my port. I show him the infection pictures of the removal of my port in September 2016. He says "That won't happen." I say, "Okay," and off to surgery we go. I wake up hurting. I could feel a lot of trauma this time. I'm in a lot of pain. I am ready to go home. Go to sleep and rest up. The same pull feeling in my neck and port area. Oh yes, I remember this pain and pulling. I know I need this port. It doesn't mean I have to like it, but it will save my life.

Everyone has been so supportive; they are having my back. Some days, I wake up and I just say, "No more." I remember how Dr. A. saved my ass, put me back together. All who went beyond to clean me; all the friends whose prayers and words encouraged me to keep going. My God gave me the ability to wake up every day. Just breathe, one breath at a time. Without air in my lungs, I have nothing. I keep remembering what I was told: "You don't have to like it, but you have to accept it."

Tuesday: meet with PA-R at Dr. S. office. He will explain to me and S O all about the 3 kinds of chemo I will have: the risks, the outcomes, the things that will make me sick, nausea pills, and how to deal. This sounds a lot like 22 years ago (1995-1996). A six hour treatment every three weeks. Long days and, I hope, good evenings. I'll lose my hair again, for the third time. I've lost 40 pounds. My healing is going well. I feel better and am starting to eat.

So all in all, a good day. God gets me through every day and holds my hand through it all and, again, has my back.

Thursday: chemo day. My nerves are at high. Everyone says be strong, you can do this, you got this. I'm so tired of hearing this. I know they all mean well. But I feel trapped inside my body. I can't get out, stuck, bound, kidnapped. I would love to be able to run. Do what I want. No driving, no lifting, no strain, no this, no that, NO, NO, NO...

I'm quiet, into myself. Feeling still, scared, I just want to cry. But I can't. So I keep it in, only to You. You can do this.

I'm doing okay. Six hours of chemo, seven bags of juice. But one down, five to go. Three weeks apart. But it will be for my healing of cancer. I'm tired, zapped, of living. So we go through and power through. Living is the goal.

Every day is a new adventure. I'm so tired today and my kidney hurts, so I am drinking cranberry/apple juice and tea. It helps, but I want it to go away. So we try our best to break through all this day by day. Went to bed at 8:30pm. My body zapped, I couldn't stay up. Slept 11 hours. Needed it.

I start another day. Too bad every day is not that way. One day you sleep well, and others, you're lucky you get a few good hours. Not every day is the same. We've got the kidney under control thanks to cranberry juice (always do a mix). Forty-eight hours later, under control. The week is a good one and we move forward. Sleep is still evading me. I would love to have more sleep.

43

Another week under my belt. We go see Dr. S. on Thursday. He gives us the news. My platelets and blood work, all good. My chemo (avastin, taxatol, carboplatin) are all working together. Down for a few days, but by day five/six, I was able to pick me up and do more. I had to have God's help, to lift and push me. I planted my geraniums; my porch looks great. I cleaned my areas around my house. I walked three times around the block, which was a big challenge. But we (me and God with S O) pushed through. I need to prove that my strength will hold up and my brain would push me through. These challenges are tough, but they are our big feats to work through. Thank God, I have God to get me through every thought, every process, every strength.

As we were talking to Dr. S., we learn all my stats are good. Dr. S. is smiling; he is confident the 3 chemos are working together for my best recovery. I asked about CARIS for my DNA. Dr. S. showed us the paperwork to show this form of treatment is the best for my DNA; it fights and controls my liver polyps and the rest of my cancer in my pelvic and rectum. If any cell would be hiding, my body's DNA is fighting with these 3 chemos.

Cancer is so complex and hard to understand. Putting it all into words is difficult. I have been dealing for 22 years with cancer and I still don't get so much of the chemical compounds of how they work. Living with this is also complex. We try to listen and learn.

Our best research still is a mountain of words. We are on the correct path. I will be healed. Cancer is not going to take me out. Round three and, third time's a charm. No way are we finished. I have five more treatments, and some could be trying, tiring, and bad to get through. But with a smile, I will do my best, and my team will be there to help me. Most of all, I have God, my best friend, to guide everyone's hands and mind. He helps me to make every day a success, and I win. Thank You, Jesus.

Had a good night sleep, from 10pm to 8:30am. My little sleep helpers are working finally. I have had two full night's sleep. This is going to be a good day. I'm wanting to use my energy to get things accomplished, so I get that sleep. I am still limited in what I can do. No driving, no vacuuming, no carrying, no stretching out of range, so...

It's Mother's Day 2017. Gifts from God are "good news." Many friends saying, "Happy." It is so sweet of all of you. You know who you are. Thank you for your wishes love, you all...

Had a beautiful Mother's Day dinner with daughter #2 for sushi. We had so much food! I have an extra dinner to take home. Thank you, it was delicious...

44

Today, I went to Dr. A. for my two month checkup. I'm feeling really good, little pangs, but mostly healing well.

I am nervous. I want to start doing things again. I do know my body isn't ready for everything. Little by little, I'm starting to do many things. Vacuuming, not so much; it hurts my core. Sweeping again, small, but pulls at my core. Little at a time. Dr. A. says I need more time, step by step. Don't be in a rush, you had major surgery. Give yourself a chance to heal. This is not going to happen overnight, but I wish it would...

The weather is changing, and the sun is shining. Rain has slowed, cool has turned to warmth. God, thank You. Spring is here and summer is hanging on the tip. Today is going to be a good day.

S O has been so angry. I guess a lot is on his plate. Me and the everyday BS. At night, he is just angry. All the words he is saying are not positive and I'm worried he's just overwhelmed. I'm hoping it's that. We rely on each other; that's what we do. Words cut and hurt. I have given it to God to change this and I've talked to S O to try and understand. At times, we all need some help, friends to be our guides. We all have our angels and I'm asking them to show the right direction. God gives us so much, and we as humans don't remember the advantages we have on earth. Peace of mind; a choice yes or no. We take for granted the things we do every day, the things God gives us to do and allows us to do every day. It's hard for humans to take a step outside of ourselves and see through the mirror of life looking back at ourselves. We all should take time to do this. Maybe learning a new skill would be helpful.

Had the most wonderful visit from our friend C. He is like family, a member we choose to have. A wonderful person. We love him. He was a welcome face. We hadn't gotten together in over a year. We had lunch; I made crab cakes and soft-shell crabs. He stayed a few hours and then went on his way. I sent him with the extra crab cakes so he would enjoy them.

Thanks, C, for spending time with S O and me! It was a good time, a nice way to spend a Saturday.

45

Sunday morning, I woke up to my head, hair follicles hurting. Hurts to touch them. Took my shower and the reason everything hurt, my hair fell out. Three weeks almost out of chemo. Yep, my hair due to leave me; 99.9% out just a few left for me to buzz. I will. I wish the whole thing would have just let go. All gone, totally bald. After my next chemo, I'm sure it probably will. Shine my head. I'm not real happy. Doesn't mean I have to like it, but have to accept it. It's a long trip and hurtful one. Not so happy. Smiles not on this face today.

Day two need to buzz the rest. My buzzer, of course, is not working. Need to go borrow one. Crap, really! It went well. Got it done and it looks much better. Now my head is freezing. Ski hat on, wish this rain would go away. Need some warmth.

Day three, still angry. You would think that after my third cancer, and my third chemo, losing my hair for the third time, I would be okay. NOT. I guess I'm just getting tired of this disease; cancer be done!

Blood work today. Check to see if I'm okay for chemo on Thursday. Woke up sad. No matter how you see it, you have no idea how my inner body feels. I am bald, I have cancer. I am going through this alone, yes alone. I have my friends, my loved ones, concerned by all. But not one of them can really understand how my heart, head, and body feels. They feel SORRY for me. I don't want your sorrow. I want your understanding. Not your sad looks, your sad touch. Stop talking and listen; you are not listening. You are not seeing. Please just STOP, STOP...

I do not need you to think you know what is best for me. Hey, guys, this is round number three, 1995-2015-2017! Do you get it, #3!? I need to be finished. I need to be able to move on. I love you all, but really, guys. Sometimes just being quiet is what I want. Please do what I asked, not what you think. You do not live in my body. So back off. Have any of you ever been bald? Let alone, round #3 cancer? Have any of you shaved your head to feel and live bald? Of course not. Did you even ask? I would have said, "NO, DON'T." But you didn't even ask. I wonder!

Yes, I am pissed! I have a right to be. Maybe you should be silent and watch; sometimes looking and seeing can give you more than you think. If you choose to, STOP, LOOK, LISTEN. Put someone else first and take a breath. Use my breath. It's warm and you may feel some of my pain. Or maybe not! Do you want to? Do you even want to try? I think not. I should feel sorry for you, that you can't. That you are the one who is losing out on this great and wonderful person. Outside looks okay, but did you really look at the interior? The windows are open, the door is see-through glass. But you are the one afraid to do that extra step. So go ahead, hold back, because you will be the one to miss this "ME." That is your fault. How else do I say it? I am special. What part of that don't you get?

46

Lately, I feel like I am always waiting on other people on their way to help me. Why can't people ever be on time? Again, this isn't about you. If I didn't want or need your help, I wouldn't ask. Maybe you're getting tired of helping me. I get that. I am tired of this, too! Again, this is my journey. I asked you along, but not to smother me. To help me. To be supportive of me. To help with the strength I didn't have and may not have. So why are you so hard to communicate with and let me down?

You may not think so, but did you ever think of why I say "okay" so much? I know if I ever really open my mouth, you wouldn't get it. I don't have the time or want to be your hand holder when I'm the one who needs MY hand held. But I just say "okay," my head feeling so sad for you. Your tunnel vision is your sad day. You should really start looking beyond. The world is a big place—not just your realm, for your own energy.

47

Day four, chemo day. Getting ready for my six hour, seven bags, of life-healing chemo. Today is long, it's tiring, it's what I need to heal me, to keep me alive. Hope I sleep a lot, get through, and have a good injection. All goes through my port, into veins, through my body. Blood counts are good. but found out I have a bladder infection. Could be meds, or who knows, but I have it. I'm also going for CT scan. I've been in some pain. Pelvic area and my rectal, these are the same areas that I had pain in when I found my cancer again. So I am nervous.

Have to drink contrast. Sometimes it bothers me, and my stomach is a little nauseous, from something I ate. At least I think so, let alone chemotherapy. So double turning two triple whammy. I need to just get through and take my nausea meds to relax my body. Go to bed, to get ready for CT scan tomorrow.

Day five. Woke up today. Slept well: 10 hours! Again, my voice is raspy. After number two chemo, only lasted a few days, last time. Using my nausea pills is a blessing. Being able to eat and keep it down, that feeling is more than most can understand. Today is CT day. Drink the contrast.

Makes me nauseous, so I hope the pills will work on that, as well. I just want answers. Going through this. When pain, complex, something I can't or shouldn't fit in comes to drag me down, I trust God. I want Him to show the truth. By truth, I can move forward. I've always been given truth upfront and I can handle what is to come next.

Nervous, yes, but confident. I know the truth will come out. I'm hoping it's just more healing pain, but to be sure, we will do the CT scan.

As we go forward with chemo, we also learn I have a bladder infection. Dr. S. listened, and I go for this CT scan Friday. Next day, the results: perforated bowel. Not good, that's the pain. Talk to Dr. S. on the phone and then the technician to get all the answers as I'm lying there having the CT scan. I go on antibiotics and have God to do the rest. Heal me, God. You got this one!

My antibiotics are working. I'm feeling somewhat better, have many days left. The pain is better and my body reacted to the antibiotics, so that is good. I need a break, need to be done with all of this. Asking for many prayers. I know God is the King and rules all.

Dr. S. called this morning to see how I was feeling. I do feel better, my pain is not as much, thankful for the antibiotics. The rest has made a difference, my discharge has lessened. It was really scary! *An infection is one thing that can kill you.* We as people sometimes don't know the height of the infection. We think that with a few cleanings and antibiotics, all will go away. When you are dealing with infection internally, that's a different item. Internal gets hidden/not noticed until it could be too late. Again, I thank God He has taught me to know my body, when it hurts and is not its normal self. This has been my clock in my lifetime to be saved. I can only urge you all to listen to what your body is telling you. To get your doctor to listen to you. Telling him or her how you feel. No one knows your body better than you, being your own advocate. Be your best advocate, always.

48

There are some days you wake up and know the day is just going to be shit! Some of the people around you are off and mean. You try your best to keep your mouth quiet and everyone snaps. There should be no blame. We all have bad days. The best thing to do is walk away. Be alone, put yourself in your mind, and move on. It's hard.

I know I've needed a lot of help and I have relied on many. If you are in a bad mood and it's your day to help me and you don't want to, please tell me; we can schedule another day. It's okay, because when you show up mad, no one has a good day. Words are said, so next time, stay home and take care of your own shit. I'll see you the next time.

We all have had a bad day. Be honest, be clear, be truthful. For all of us. I don't know what you're going through. And you certainly have no idea what I'm going through. I don't want you to walk in my shoes. You couldn't handle it. Nor do I want you to. This is my journey. I ask for your help, not to berate me to tears. Think next time and don't come.

49

Today, I saw Dr. S., got my Xarelto. I'm feeling better, finished sulfur, have three days left on my antibiotic. Then I wait to see what Dr. A. has to say about CT scan and what we should do next. Dr. S. wants Dr. A. to read and comment on the CT scan before we decide the next step.

Woke up and had more infection discharge, so infection is not gone in the bowel. Calling Dr. S. for more antibiotics for another 10 days. That's okay. God, You are the only one who can really make this go away.

Then to beat all, I wake up today and the bladder infection is back. What the...! I call Dr. S. and he wants another antibiotic and a urine culture. We need to get to the bottom of this.

ENOUGH.

The problem is, I'm getting chemo. Chemo is killing all cells, good and bad, to fight this cancer. Now I have two infections, giving me antibiotics, putting back good cells, making them fight this infection. We are playing with a double-edged sword: Good vs. bad. Infection vs. cherno . Antibiotics vs. cherno.

Antibiotics want new cells to heal the infection, and I do need them. But chemo is saying we need to kill all cells to fight cancer. So who wins? I need divine intervention for this one. God, please place Your hand and heal this infection...TODAY!

50

Today is Thursday, chemo day. Saw Dr. S., not going to give me Avastin, so only half a chemo, not real happy. He's afraid Avastin will stop the healing of my bowel.

Today is Friday, I'm seeing Dr. A. He gave me a rectal internal exam, says everything is healing fine. They (others) are afraid of my bowel healing. Avastin will stop the healing or slow it down. Dr. A. said, "Go get your Avastin. Have Dr. S. give you your treatment, everything is fine." Back to Dr. S.'s office we go. I'm going to get my Neulasta shot today anyway.

Dr. A. sent text to Dr. S. They gave me my Neulasta shot; they also give me my Avastin Cherno. All in all, this was a good day.

Did 1/2 chemo: 3 bags down, now 3 bags to go. Perfect, schedule is back on track. God took a sad day and turned it in a magical day! God keeps teaching me not all things are bad or look bad. My faith must get stronger, my love of

God is always strong, and my heart is full, glowing, beaming. Being human, I'm still learning. Human is mind, body, chemical, flesh. My angel inside is holding me together to give my God His right in my life.

Thank You, Jesus, for Your love for me. As I write "God picked me" again, I can feel Him telling me, "Smile, you deserve it."

51

Some days I get so confused, I think this really can't be happening again. Twenty-two years and I'm back at cervical/endometrial cancer. Why did it come back? It went away, or stayed dormant, but why did it come back? I want to believe for research not to kill me, then my human side takes over and says, "You are no big deal." But my godly side says, "YES, you are. You are a very big deal. God made you, you accepted, you picked your journey, as you said 'HARD.'" But now is very hard. I know God has a big, loving outcome for His work. I'm just His sculpture, He is the artist. I don't know what to think, how to react, how to follow, but I'm doing my best.

Cancer is hard. It hurts, it shames, it belittles, it makes emotions I can't even describe. You are living with a disease and you can't say, "Away, I don't want to do this anymore." You go through so many steps that take you through so many journeys, your brain freezes. You lose thought, forget mid-sentence, try to pick up where you lost the thought, but can't. My friends called it "CHEMO BRAIN." The worst is, you are told "that doesn't happen." Hey you, try this and tell me this doesn't happen! Well, I am here to tell you it does. Try living it. A thought comes, you're talking, and you just forget where your thought went. GONE. It may take thoughts from you, or the person you are talking to, to get it back. You laugh, and both have a good laugh. You do wonder: does this go away? Does it stay on after chemo is over? As I get older, can this harm me? I don't know. These are wonderings only God can clean up and have the exact answers for. I'm praying for a strong healthy brain to return.

Many things go through my brain. I know I'm a good person. I try to do my best. Doesn't always turn out the way I envisioned, but that is human life. We all know one day, we will all atone for our missed opportunities, or if you wish, SINS.

I hope we can all learn lessons. Thank God for His hand in our human life as God and you have seen fit for your daily adventure. Grace to us all. Health to all and those in need.

God does forgive, all you need to do is ask. *God does listen*, I am proof, as are you.

Keep your journey, known in your heart what is your path. You can choose. Pick wisely. Help those who need your advice, your hand, your help. It comes back to you ten-fold. God loves us all, always.

52

I't's Monday, after a long hard weekend. Had chemo Thursday/Friday, two days in a row. My body is wiped out. It hurts so much, don't touch me. I just want to stay in one position and not move. Knowing it's not good for me, I'm moving. It really hurts. Trying to explain is very difficult. You feel like you have the worst flu, you can't move your joints. Your body—every bone, muscle, vein—every part just aches. Your vision is compromised, you see blurriness. You feel that you could fall. Your equilibrium is way off. You just want to feel better and you can't. Sleeping in one position, your body doesn't want you to move in any direction, your body just hurts too much.

Thank goodness I have pills to help me sleep. I sleep 12 hours, that's a great night. Then I get up to start the same routine all over again. Maybe 2, 3, 4 days of this. I never knew how long each treatment takes to absorb in my body. I know it hurts. Yes, it's killing all my cancer cells. I have to believe that. What you go through is just as hard.

Don't feel sorry for me. Pray for me. Help God heal me. Our prayers are needed and wanted. We hold on to them and they carry us through our hard times. Just knowing my family, friends, people I don't know are praying for me makes every day a blessing. I/we go through this cancer process and learn to have compassion, strength, and great emotion for what I/we/they are going through.

Thanking you all, thanking God. Looking at the sky is a comfort. The heat of the sun, the pillowy clouds, the blue of the world spinning helps.

So, THANK YOU ALL. REALLY, THANK YOU.

Today has been a long week: drained, out of sorts, equilibrium off, wobbly, like the flu hit me. Like I am coming down off an illness. But guess what, this is chemo. The hurts were heightened mass. They were so high I couldn't be touched. "Don't touch me."

This is a common thing when dealing with chemo. Poison running through your veins. It's our understanding. You have no idea of this unless you're going through this personally. Cancer is something most people can't and don't want to know. They look at you as "you poor thing" or "glad it's not me." But, guess what, it could be any of us, you included. Do you get it now? Cancer victims are HEROS, all HEROS. Most people would crawl up in a ball and just hide your heads. Scream or cry. All of which we HEROS have done. Give us more credit because we deserve it!

53

Thursday, chemo day

This is chemo #4. All went well. Got my bags of juice, 5½ hours this time. My treat after was a vanilla milkshake and a slice of pizza. Felt good to eat. I even slept okay.

Got a call from another doctor, a urologist, Dr. C., and went to see him. He was nice. I have a stent in my bladder to my kidney. It has been giving me so much discomfort, pain. It doesn't like being in my body. It has been 2 months and I feel like I have an infection. Dr. C. reports urine check says no to infection. I ask him to please do a culture to make sure. He's not happy, but he does. Comes back and *it is an infection*. One thing I have learned: be your own advocate. You know your body better than anyone does, listen to your body. Dr. C. gives me an antibiotic and make another appointment.

We are talking. Dr. C. is very interested in my case.

Tells me that I'm an odd case, he has never heard of endometrial/cervical cancer coming back even after 20 years. I said to him, "I have been told this many times!"

Thank You, God, for this change and appointment. Thank you!

Day 2 after chemo (Saturday)

Achy and tired. Slept 12 hours. My brain wants to do so much, but my body won't let me. I'm lucky, I can get up to pee! Sit still and keep your head up. Be strong, do what you can. Don't push too hard. Don't get hurt or fall. Relax. Rest, your body is asking for this, so give it to your body.

Day 3 after chemo

Still so achy and hurting. Just hurting! No energy, no nothing. Rest and relax, that's all I can do. So, I am.

Day 4 after chemo

Still achy: no energy. Again, rest, relax, don't push. Try your best.

Going back to see Dr. C. (urologist) after talking to Dr. A. We came to the sense of taking out the stent. It's causing infection/bacteria, so it needs to come out. It's been in over 4 months, and Dr. A. feels that time is enough, so out it will come. We need to wait 3 more weeks to see if all is healed. Thank You, God, they are finally listening to me, hearing our concerns. Thank You for making them listen. Only You could do this. Thank You.

Back to Dr. C. It has been 3 weeks. The stent gets taken out tomorrow at 9am. Thank You, God, for making this possible. All things came together for my good. God said YES and used the doctors to bring the answers of good.

My stent was removed, and I'm feeling better already. My pain is slowing, my bacterial infection is under control, the antibiotics are working, my brain and body are happy. Thank You, God.

Day 3 after stent removal

My body is feeling so much better. It feels free from pain I have been feeling for 2 months since my infection started. My body and I are very happy.

Thanking God for giving me His grace, and the glory goes to my God. Thank You, thank You, thank You.

Chemo day

I can't believe it has been 20 days already; this time has flown by so fast. Again, it's chemo time. Chemo #5. Now it's the end of July 2017; summer is almost ⅔ over.

Had my 5th bout of chemo. Went well. So much better now that the stent has been removed. My pain level down to a 2, just the usual aches and pains due to chemo. No more pain in my bladder, kidney, uterus. Relieved the stent is out. Moving my body, legs, waist, bending, up and down, stretching my legs. Just moving it feels great and easy!

Thank You, God, for curing my body. I know the stent had to come out. My body was rejecting the stent; it'd had enough. God has brought many body part wonderings to my mind, understanding how they work, and as the stent was getting more painful and the antibiotics were not working, I knew my body was rejecting this stent. So out it had to come. Within 6 hours after the stent was removed, it was 100% better. Relating these facts to me so now I understand. Within days, my body was able to reclaim this painless effect on the rest of my aches and my kidneys were back to normal. I knew God's perfect wisdom is in charge for my benefit. THANK YOU, GOD!

54

Thursday #5 Chemo Day

Blood work: good.
Kidney: normal (as I knew it would be). So glad God's power is in charge.

Six and a half hours of chemo, again, without much pain. I'm feeling better.

Day 3 after chemo

Achy, fatigued, tired, but pain level, low. So much to be thankful for. Hope my time leaving out will be shorter, due to not much pain. Prayers to God and many thank you.

Day 6 after chemo

Achy, tired, fatigued, the usual. Better, but not yet. Shaky today, but I can handle this.

Thank You, God, for having our backs. Angels on our shoulders. Grateful for Your love, our connection, unbreakable.

Had a dream or thought to tell people....

"LET YOUR HEART SMILE."

Someone close needs to hear , they can , "LET THEIR HEART SMILE." Even when we feel stressed, over-whelmed, closed in, we need to "LET OUR HEARTS SMILE." God wants you to, and we need it as humans. To allow ourselves, to forgive ourselves. Most of all, allow our "HEARTS TO SMILE."

55

Chemo number 6

This is my last treatment in my series of chemo. Hoping all will be a go!

Had my 5½ hours of chemo. Slept through most of my treatment; it was my first time doing that. When I came home, fell asleep for another two hours. My body needed the rest. The big information comes on Friday; I get to see Dr. A. and discuss when I get my colostomy reversed, set up the scans to see my interior organs and find out where my cancer-polyps are. I'm praying all are gone.

Friday

Day to see Dr. A. for exam. My internal check out (boy, that hurt) and Dr. A. said all felt great. Five weeks before anything can be done. Chemo needs to settle in my body, give it a chance to do the job of killing cells. My appointment for surgery is Monday, 9/18/17. I am hoping that all these tests show that it is reversal time! Dr. A. is going to open me up again to visually see what my interior is looking like. Many of my scans have given a false positive answer, often saying, "Yes, all is good," when things were not.

Makes me very nervous to hear that the scans can be false. I feel my body is ready for this long five months of healing and treatment, for worry to be over. I know it is God's day to predict, but my heart is aching for a perfect answer. God doesn't do junk; He is perfection and He uses my doctors to get me to His perfection. Thank You, God.

9/17/17

We just went through Irma, the biggest hurricane in all time! Thank You, God, for Your miracle in saving Key West. Saving so many. We needed Your help and called for Your salvation.

56

Many things called progressing. I finished my chemo and waited out the five weeks for chemo to settle in my body. I went to have barium bowel test. I can't describe to you the invasion you feel, but it must be done. Took over an hour, x-rays, tube up your butt, fluid squeezed in, and you're on candid camera. Surgery to be reversed, Monday, 9/18/17. Happy this part will be over, colostomy reversed! Guess what, ha ha ha, you're wrong.

I knew I had a fistula, perforation (basically, a hole in my bowel) on the lower end. It's been there a few months. Doctors were worried about it. Could have been caused by Avastin chemo, or an infection, anything interfering with my healing. It happened, so in comes the hole. Won't heal on its own. Surgery is scheduled for a reattachment/another repair. You can't have a hole in your bowel if you want a working bowel. We change course, get me in to have this extensive surgery to be another part of the process to being a whole human again.

God is my strength and I need Him every day to hold me up, take my fear, and see me through. One day at a time. It's a long road. But I'll make it. God told me He has my back. I believe Him, so to surgery we go.

We made it home. I thought the ride would kill me. My ass hurts, so much surgery on your lower bowel, stretching your anus. Instruments up your cavity and then not being able to sit, stand, or breathe. The pain is so bad, one drug makes you constipated, another induces bleeding. By the fourth day, I'm off meds.

It has been 10 days and the pain is still up my ass. One day lighter, the next day heavy. I try to make it the best I can or lay still. The pain just rests. My body has been in constant pain for six months! If it's not surgery, it's stent, or it's infection. Surgery again, internals, checking healing, chemo. It's time to stop. Not yet, I haven't been reversed. It doesn't look like it's going to be very soon.

Today is CAT scan day. My body is not happy, drinking contrast. Poured in but lost as soon I drank it. Running to the bathroom to empty the bag, tummy not a happy player either. Have my CAT scan for my pelvic, abdomen, liver. Please let this cancer be gone. Please let chemo work. My nerves are at high, my ass hurts. My tears streaming down my face. All I can ask is God, please help me. All will be right! I am not a good waiter, time is so long. The sun is shining, my super friend L and I are texting. She calms me, gets me back to reality, changes my thoughts. It was a good chat with L. God knew what I needed, and L gave it to me. Thank You, God.

This is painful anger, driven by pain so real and large that every day I'm overwhelmed. So much pain, my body doesn't want to go on. My brain, my heart, my body, my God-given life. It all says you need to stay strong, pray. There are times that I just want to scream and say I'm done. I know my God would be disappointed in me for giving up, so I don't.

I know God can take my pain, my cancer away in a snap of His fingers. Why I'm not free of this, only God knows. I live here on earth as a human. I am God's angel and I know one day, my wings will show again. Not today. I feel them, know they are there. Today is not wing day. I'm starting to go stir crazy!

It has been four weeks since my anus surgery. Dr. A. said he did a chain stitch, 360°, around. My pain is at 6 to 11, but if I drugged up, I'm nothing (but a mess). It's a pain to deal with. Once in a while, I take ½ a morphine or oxycodone pills to help. That barely covers the number 6 to 11 pain. Moving forward, it's what this is about, so moving on.

57

I t has been five weeks out of surgery, the pain in my ass, ha ha. Finally, I'm feeling a bit better and my pain is lowered to a 3 to 5, not an 8 to 11. Still taking ½ a morphine pill. Can't believe this pill is finally working, but I'm not a pill popper. Pain is pain, intense is beyond.

Week six and pain is diminished further. Thank You, God. Healing more now. I know this may seem trivial to some, but pain can ruin your life. Constant pain is exhausting! It takes everything to get through and deal with the day. Getting out of pain is my goal and being able to be a functioning human. Pain is so stressing and can take you out of everything.

Week seven. Diminishing pain almost to the point of none! Not completely, but it's my way. Pain is less, pain pills are not necessary for me anymore. I have my God, my Father, my Creator, my Strength, healing me. Thank You, my God.

58

Thursday, I start Keytruda, 11/16/2017. As Dr. S. put it, "I have high molecular burdens," a good candidate for Keytruda.

Out of something bad, is something wonderful. Doctors had me mixed up with someone else. She was not doing well and had a stroke. Wasn't me, but now she is doing fine.

I got my results of blood work/stats. All perfect. My levels are high: my kidney, my thyroid, my lungs, my liver. Yes, my liver! All functioning perfect. Even with cancer in my liver, it is still functioning the best it can. They said "PERFECT." That is why I love my God, His perfect ways. Relying on His answers. Thank you all for your prayers.

God only does perfect. Thank You, God. Thank You for all my people praying for me. All these prayers for me! Keep all your prayers coming, I send many to all people and ask for them to send more to me.

59

ENCOUNTER #6

Again God reminded me of this dream

I was having a dream one night. God came to me and said these words:

"Come to Me with open arms. My arms will always be there. Come to Me and hold Me tight. My arms will never fail."

I woke up, I knew I had to write them down. They are compelling and give me strength. Thank You, God.

This is my second time for God to remind me of this verse...strange it is a year later...

PART III

60

I t's Friday. I saw Dr. A. All my healing is going well. Dr. A. feels I need some more healing. Six more weeks, but that's okay, I can do this. I've been told I can go on vacation! YAY, so we will go and check out Key West! My S O and I will be on our way. All the problems are put aside for a few weeks. We will go and relax. I'm so needing and wanting this time. It has been eight months since my surgery in March. I've been in so much pain. *This time will be so treasured and blessed.* S O and I are very happy. Water, warmth, sun, beach. Thank You, God.

Keytruda infusion #5. My stats and blood work were excellent. All in the high range of good, excellent. My organs are in the high-to-perfect range again. My liver is full of cancer: 5 holes, 2 on the left, 2 on the right, 1 in the center. Somehow it is functioning in the perfect range, blood flowing through this imperfect liver. In my eyes, God's perfect way to tell me that He is in control and has my back, He is my perfect way, and He alone can change everything. Even a cancer in my liver. God's timing is my life.

61

ENCOUNTER #7

December 2017

Here is where encounter number 7 begins.
Again in a dream:

I know I am sleeping, human sleeping. Sleeping and dreaming in my dream. Many things are rushing through my mind, but still know that I know I am asleep. Dreaming within a sleep and dreaming. Trying to figure out what I'm supposed to be doing.

God and I are communicating, though. I knew He was speaking to me, racing in my mind. I know this, but am trying to make sense of all these thoughts. Much like any other dream, but I know there is significant knowledge I need to understand. Trying to get the process going, to understand, when all of a sudden, I wake up from the intense dream.

Woke up in my human dream knowing my answer to all of these thoughts. God gave me the title of the book: *GOD PICKED ME.*

Again, this is so profound, I begin to have tears roll down my cheeks, and I smile. My heart is bursting with joy. I have longed for this, for months. Almost feeling guilty for not having a title. I should already know, God's timing not mine! Again, thank You, God.

In closing, I hope I will be able to be proud. That I have been able to use this God-given time. It helps me to keep growing, use my focus, think more clearly. Be thankful, use my manners, say yes. Say thank you, say I'm sorry, say I love you. Say I can help.

All of this has been bestowed on ME. It's time to pay it forward. Thank you for reading. Thank You, God.

62

We start all over again. We are home from our vacation. Had a wonderful time! Rested, relaxed, and got some vitamin D in my bones.

It's Monday. This week is full of doctor appointments, tests, blood work, and hopefully good results.

I see Dr. S. on Tuesday. Dr. S. says my stats and blood work are great. My markers are at the lowest they have been. This is super news. All organs, kidneys, lungs, liver are in perfect function range. More super news. Dr S. sets up a PET scan for Wednesday, 1/24/2018. I go have this done. Radiation again, infusion...

It's Thursday, and Dr. A. sets up Barium Enema test #2 for 1/25/2018. I have had this test before, also called a leak test. It's a terribly invasive test. Has to be done to see if the Fistula is gone or if I'm leaking in any way. Check for the reversal of my colostomy. I'm hoping/praying for this. I can feel my body is ready for me to be put back together. My heart and brain are ready. Is the rest of me?

The test is crazy! A probe is put up your rectum and a balloon is inflated. It hurts. But this helps the barium liquid to go through the bowel track into your intestines. It goes into my colostomy bag: good sign, it's working. It's going through my intestines, when all of a sudden there is barium everywhere. It's all over the place: the table I'm lying on, me. And, oh, the panic. But we proceed. Have to get this finished and get the photos. It's only liquid; we can clean it up.

The test now over, the doctor is satisfied he has enough for the results. I'm left lying in barium on the table. The nurses scatter, telling me not to move, so I stay still. They come back with towels and stuff me full, help me up, get to the bathroom and start my clean up. To my surprise, the waffle adhesive has let go. The waffle is part of my colostomy bag that adheres to my skin. It holds everything in place. It has loosened and the barium is running out... thank God it's nothing to do with the test! I clean myself up the best I can, tell the nurse what has happened. Relieved, she is okay with this. Says she will explain to the doctor. Yes, the test is done.

I go straight home. I need to shower to get this barium off me. S O and I put another colostomy attachment on me again. What a day! All the time, praying that all will be okay with the test. I don't want to have to go through this again.

It's Friday, 1/26/2018. I haven't heard from Dr. S. It has been the longest 24 hours to wait for test results. Just as I was calling Dr. S., he answers his phone and says, "I was just picking up my phone to call you! I have great news for you: YOUR CANCER IS GONE!" I asked if this was true and he replied, "I'M OVER THE MOON! Not only is your cancer gone, your liver is healing and rejuvenating. The holes in your liver have gotten drastically smaller and are closing."

I can't even explain the joy and surprise I am feeling! My heart and my body are beaming with joy. We talk for a few minutes and I tell him, "THIS IS GOD'S MIRACLE!" *Not just because my cancer is gone, but my liver is healing, rejuvenating.* The holes are closing. They are smaller. Only God can create a miracle like this. I was told when the cancer is under control/gone, it would take YEARS for holes to close and heal. As I said, "ONLY GOD." Only He could create this miracle to happen. I am so blessed to have this happen in my life. "THANK YOU, GOD!"

We end our conversation, both thanking God, and the tears of joy start streaming down my cheeks. My S O and I are in awe. Speechless, I call my girls, friends, loved ones, and all who have prayed and seen me through almost 2 years of this cancer. I thank you all, each one of you. All who have been in my circle to help make this miracle a reality. Words are still caught in my throat. My heart is glowing with my love from God to have "PICKED ME," as my book is titled. "GOD PICKED ME" and "GOD PICKED ME AGAIN."

What more can I say? I have been in God's hands for so long and He has held me so tight to not let me go. To carry me through this. To have my back, He told me. This is a MIRACLE ! I, and all around me, cannot deny this. Thank You, God.

I'm not finished yet. Cancer is gone. I still have my colostomy and Dr. A. feels the test went well, but wants to give my body another 3 months to heal. He doesn't want to invade my body so soon after the news of my cancer being gone and my liver healing. I'm disappointed, but I understand the reasoning. My body is healing from major surgery and shock. Heal we will, and I'll see Dr. A. in February 2018. He will check me, and in April, we revisit this option to reverse me again. Healing is my goal, and my power to be a whole human again.

Time it is and heal I will.

It has been three weeks and I'm still in awe of the most wonderful news. I can only and will only give the healing power to God. Prayers and positive energy. Thank You, God.

63

ENCOUNTER #8

March 20, 2018

I keep asking God why this was happening. Really needing, wanting, to understand His plan. Trying to adjust. On Monday, March 20, 2017, I woke up and jotted down this dream—encounter #8.

I had gone to bed still feeling uneasy, anxious, my mind not at ease. The night was pretty, the moon bright, waking from a dream or still in a dream state. But asking God for His perfect answer.

I have this feeling: I'm lying on my right side, covers on, quietly asking, "God, who am I? What is this all about?" I can't move, my body is frozen. *We talk.*

God tells me I'm His angel and I wanted to come to earth to see how humans live. He gives me a choice as to what and how to make this life: hard/easy/so so. He asks for my answer and I say, "HARD." Then hard, it is. I know I'm in God's great presence and doing God's will. Not perfect, not always correct, but I'm 64 years old, trying to be faithful, encouraging, sometimes feeling great, others not understanding cancer, but knowing I must move forward. I asked! Human I am. My godly will. I know God loves me, His eternal blessing.

He tells me He will never leave me, I am not alone, and He will always have my back. Being God's child, trusting His hands, and trusting His love. Beating this human mind, I wake up. Thank You, God, for allowing me (Your angel) *grace and will!*

I remember lying there, and my mind wants to remember every detail. I am not able to move; nothing but my eyes, like I am paralyzed. Still talking, my conversation with God. He knows me, my sense of learning, *my need for HIM.*

So now I must take this encounter, this dream, and realize what I have been given. Take this gift and try to do the best every human can do.

64

I saw Dr. A. It's April and he wants to wait till May. After my exam, he still felt my many stitches.

Again, I am put off till September. I do understand, because healing is the most important thing. I need to be thoroughly healed.

Healing is the key. He also could feel the fistula and wants to give it more time to heal, as well. So heal we will.

65

As I sit here waiting for winter to be over and spring to arrive, I'm reminded of the past 2 years of cancer and surgery and pain and healing. Thankfully, our bodies are able to forget the struggle, the effort we put into the healing process. We really don't forget what we went through. We forgive: the energy, the helplessness, and the agony of getting to this spot of wellness. We want to remember everything so we can explain the courage it took to get to this amazing change. This change happening to your bodies, hearts, minds. We need to experience this whole system of life to be able to hold on to the good and the discomfort.

God in His powerful grace gives us the ability to move forward and find joy in our hearts, moving forward from the pain, hurt, sorrow, frailty, discomfort. He is our only guide to allow us the ability to move through this stage in our human/earthly life. Giving my energy to negative thoughts only made it harder to have this cancer. I realized the power I had through God. The aspect of getting through became sensitive to my being. I could hold my power to accept this cancer that embodied my life and find a clear path to the most miraculous end. I'M ALIVE and I'M HEALING, rejuvenating one of the most important organs for all humans to survive, the liver. I know this didn't happen all on its own. My team of doctors (brains and hands), radiation, chemotherapy, knowledge of Keytruda, and my faith in God helped perform the miracle I needed to live.

I have been told many times, "YOU CAN'T LIVE WITHOUT A LIVER." My liver is rejuvenating, as well as healing. "IT IS A MIRACLE." I can't say it enough. You don't have to believe, but I am living this miracle. I also have to praise my circle for prayers, friends, doctors, loved ones, and God.

The Word of God says, "When two or more come together and pray, it shall be done." Well, I am that miracle, and I will always believe this happened. I am this living proof.

God TOLD ME to write my book. *Yes, told me.* So I am. I am special to God. He told me that, too! So I listened and did as He asked.

God wants us all to be happy, healthy, and kind. things I'm still learning to do better at. Trying to make a difference. "WHY ME?" I don't ask anymore. Now I say, "WHY NOT ME?"

I love You, God, and thank You for picking me. As my title says, "GOD PICKED ME."

That is how I roll today. I was picked and I'm proud to be able to say, "I was picked", not once, not twice, but every day I breathe.

66

I t has been several months now and I have been doing
my Keytruda, having my checkups, doing all my work
on healing. I get my Keytruda every 3 weeks. It has been a
very good infusion in my recovery. Keytruda is an
immunotherapy drug. It is used on cancer patients for
many types of cancers, mine being endometrial/cervical.
Me, I'm doing great with Keytruda. It is helping me live
through my cancer battle. But the best part is, me/we/my
family/team of doctors are winning this battle. My team is
so strong. I know I could not have made it through these
past few years without all of their expertise and friendship. I thank them with all my heart, soul, and being.

If I didn't have my God in my life, my saving Grace, my
best friend, there is not a second that goes by that I cannot
give Him. God, the Glory for the miracles of my healing.
His miracles of me being alive. His miracles of putting the
correct doctors in my path to carry me through this
ordeal. We found my common ground and we all are

working for my life. It also helps that my team of doctors, nurses, helpers, family, friends, and loved ones love the knowledge of God and the miracles He is shining in my life of recovery. It has been a long journey (not ended yet), but we are seeing the path and leading each other down it. As always, thank You, Jesus, my God.

67

It's Friday, May 18, 2018. Dr. A. day and checkup. My stomach is in knots, nervous, and I'm shaking. Only my heart knows the news will be good. My S O and I head toward Dr. A.'s office in the pouring rain. We check in, sit, wait my turn. They call me. I see the staff and our greetings are nice and pleasant. Thank you.

He knocks and comes in, does my exam. Thoroughly. I mean *thorough*. Feeling, pushing, making sure my body is completely examined. Now for the results. They are good. He says that my stitches have healed, finally. My fistula is still there, but smaller. My tissue healed well. My scar tissue, "IT'S GONE." He is amazed (as I had a lot of scar tissue from all my surgeries I have had). He is smiling and his voice sounds excited. That has always been my way of knowing his thought—if I'm good or if something is wrong. I'm very happy for this result. We are moving forward and my healing is great. So smiles all around.

68

Now the start of trying to get me back. I still have my colostomy. It has been a long road. I have said, "My heart goes out to all who have to have a colostomy for the rest of their lives." I feel for them. I feel lucky, I have had mine for 15 months and it does feel like forever, but I know it's not. It has been longer than was supposed to be. My healing was slower and longer than expected, along with the second surgery to reattach my bowel area. It made things longer and slower. In all, I always say, "I'M BREATHING."

I have to go to a new gastroenterologist, as my fistula is still causing wait time. My heart is telling me it's gone, but my tests results say it's still there, in my bowel/rectal area. To another doctor, Dr. M., we go! We drive to Sinai Hospital in Baltimore, a 2 hour drive to see him. Dr. A. calls him the Guru of Stents. The traffic is crazy, as usual, as we arrive. We sit for an hour before being called. Now it's our turn. We go into our room, vitals are taken, questions are asked/answered. The nurse says, "The nurse practitioner will be in shortly." I'm astonished. (I didn't drive all this way to see a nurse practitioner.)

I say, "I'm here to see Dr. M." They say, "He had an emergency and was called out of the office this morning." I look at the nurse and say, "Wait a minute, you're telling me he was called out this morning to do emergency surgery. It is now 3:30pm in the afternoon, and you didn't call me to reschedule?" Nurse says, "It was felt that the NP could see you." I said, "NO, I'm not here for a simple stomach problem! I'm here to talk stent and possible surgery. Seeing the N.P. is not acceptable."

Then the nurse goes to get the office manager, K. She comes in and apologizes to me. Says, "Dr. M. must have skipped over you, and you fell through the cracks." Great. Are you kidding me!? Really.

Of course, I'm not happy. We make another appointment, 3 weeks later. The earliest that we can get. So, come back we must.

My S O and I journey back home, 4 hours. It's rush hour and traffic is large. It's 7:30pm before we walk in the front door. Exhausted and hurting from the time sitting in the car, all I want to do is go to bed! We relax a while, eat something, and at 9:30pm, my head is ready to hit my pillow.

The next day, I'm still in disbelief that they didn't have the courtesy to call me to change my appointment. I'm calling Dr. A.'s office to get nurse N. on the line. Telling her what happened, she is not happy with them either. She will explain to Dr. A., get to the bottom of this. then have Dr. A. get in touch with me.

I do hear from Dr. A. He apologizes for my troubles of the previous day's events. (I know he has nothing to do with this.) He just gives his help and encourages me to make another appointment. I already have.

I am hoping this is God's way of intervening. Hoping God is putting these blocks ahead of me so my fistula continues to heal and I would not need surgery. Only God has the power to make miracles and I have had so many. I will always take as many as God is willing to give me. Thank You, God, for giving me more.

My gut is saying go see Dr. M., listen to him and what he has to say. Also go for another barium test. Believe me, this test hurts! It is no picnic. It's invasive, but it's also necessary. As today has been eye opening in my learning to listen and hear God, I call this day, an exceptional day. The sun is shining, I am smiling.

Here we go again. Dr. M. calls me again to change my appointment. We go through the reason why I have a later appointment time. The office manager says, "I remember you, and why we have to keep a later time, so we will keep you at 11:30am." I tell her, 'You never sent me the paperwork needed, nor the address change to get there." I take the address down as to be able to put it in my GPS. I can tell she is embarrassed (again) and says sorry for the mishap. She will see me on Monday.

I'm feeling like another roadblock, more that God is interjecting His power. Thank You, Jesus. Keep it coming, Lord. I need Your input!

Wait for Monday, appointment at 11:30am.

It's Monday. We drive to Baltimore again to see Dr. M. as scheduled.

I wish I had all the time back that we have waited in many doctors' offices! Hours upon hours. On our way, S O says to me, "Please call DR. M.'s office to make sure the appointment is confirmed." I do and, behold, they changed the place back to Sinai office again without calling and telling me! Thank God S O had a brain.

We arrive and wait an hour to see Dr. M. We are placed in a room and wait. Finally, a knock at the door. Dr. M. walks in.

We shake hands. He is very nice, polite, and helpful. Knowledgeable, he knows his stuff. Dr. A. said a guru. I can see why.

He explains all of my options. What must happen before surgery?

Barium Test

View test (like a colonoscopy) using a camera to see what the fistula and insides look like. Then and only then will he be able to tell if/when I need this stent surgery.

I am happy for another barium test—not that I want this. It's my most updated information in my fistula. The barium will tell how much the fistula has healed, and if God has granted me my miracle again. This is my hope. My gut is telling me so. My faith is telling me so. So we wait till the next week for my test. One more week.

Thank You, God, for this extra week to heal and have this miracle become reality. Never give up hope. The last thing you lose is hope.

69

It's Thursday. I'm going for my 4th Barium test (at 10am), also called a leak test. As usual, everyone is so kind and nice. They feel for me, to have to keep coming back for these invasive tests. The doctor doing my test has done this test on me before. He shows me the fistula on the screen. Yes, it is still there. Damn... okay.

Not sure if it is leaking. That will be in the report. This time my pain is not so much. I have healed well and the test is bearable. Makes a difference between heavy pain and minimal pain. The test is done. I've had all the x-rays needed, cleaned up from barium, get dressed, waited for the disc (my copy of test), and I'm on my way out the door to go home. We say our goodbyes, thank you's, and as always, "I hope you don't have to go through this again." We laugh, and I say, "Me, too." I'm pissed it's not healed or gone. But, this is a process, we only can move on to the next step.

I get in my car, start off to do my errands. Get to the stop sign and my car stops also. The engine stalls. I try to start it again; no good, it won't start. Crappers, folks! Okay, calm down, try it again. The engine is trying to kick over, but it won't start. I know it is not my battery, it's not dead. Feels like it's not getting any fuel. Try it again. The same, nothing. I call my S O. He drops everything and drives the 20 minutes to come help me. I wait, stuck at the stop sign, blocking traffic. I have to wave everyone around me. Some people were nice, asked if I needed help. Others were just annoyed. Can't please everyone! Call my repair guy/friend, he tells me to have my car towed to him, his place. Dang, it isn't supposed to be this hard!.

Thank goodness, I have AAA. Give them a call. S O shows up. I tell him I called AAA; it will be a 90 minute wait. Damn, damn. I receive a call back from an AAA guy. He is kind and only 5 minutes away! Perfect. I explain where I am and where I have to go; again, my repair is 4 blocks away. So far, so good. Towman showed up with a flatbed truck, hooks my car, and it's up on the flatbed. No problems, yay. We are on our way. He knows my repair guy and is happy it is so close. We are off.

I just had my car cleaned and polished. It looks beautiful. Of course, it starts to rain! Oh, well. We are here, really 5 blocks away from where I got stuck. I walk in to see D, my repair guy. He says hi, hugs me, and says can't get to your car till next week. What am I going to do? It is what it is. Stay the course, wait for answers; for my test as well as my car. Valleys and hurdles! Okay, okay, all is good, thank You, God.

I'm in that spot. *I'm praying and wishing for clear*

answers. I know God is hearing me. He is holding me. He is my strength. Thank You, God. I'm in Your care. I feel Your hugs. I will get through this. This too shall pass. This too shall be solved. This too shall make me smile. Positive, positive power and blessings. Thank You my God...

70

I t's Thursday the following week and I don't have answers. I'm waiting for answers. I decide to call Dr. A's office to see if he can give Dr. M. a call (as doctors converse faster than we the patients get our results). Have a conversation with them and get some answers. I know God says, "When nothing is happening, God is at work." Oh please, be at work, figure this out, God, please! I'm so down, I'm pouting, and I know I'm not supposed to. I am human. I am an angel in human form. Dang, human waiting is so hard. I need to remember, God's time, not mine. Keep saying "This is NOT MINE!" Finally, a call from Dr. M. on Tuesday! He says he and Dr. A. talked and read my report, but want to look at the pictures from the disc of my test. Disc being sent to Dr. A. so he can share with Dr. M.

Step 1: Okay.
Step 2: Stent is out.

Dr. M. says stent is out, but not unhappy about stent. Didn't want it anyway, not another stent. Dr. M. says report shows my fistula is there, just there. Not attached to anything important, not my bladder, rectum, vagina, organs at all. Not hanging to cause a problem in other areas. That is great news. Dr. M. thinks it could be filled with GLUE, yes glue. He said to fill with glue, and stitched it closed. Still wants to wait to see the disc pictures first. Wait for the disc to arrive and take a look. He will study them for the best possible outcome.

I feel positive about this. We can move forward and positive to have a few answers. Thank You, God, for answering my prayers. The start of an ending to this pain in my ass... Keep praying. Time heals all pain. Answers are around the corner.

71

Wednesday, Keytruda Day.

Blood work, great. Seeing Dr. S. All labs are in the good zone. Perfect. He is very happy with them. So we move forward. I tell him about my conversation with Dr. M. and Dr. A. where I am with my fistula. Had my other barium test, again, #4. Had a disc sent to the DR's, Dr. A. and Dr. M.

They could see the pictures of my fistula and track. The fistula is not gone, but it is NOT attached to anything vital—no organs, my bladder, my vagina, my rectum. The pocket fistula in the track of my bowel, so that has not changed and is not moving or attaching to anything else in my interior. That is a very good sign. The result is good. It is about 3 centimeters (1½ inches length), 2 centimeters (1 inch width). It is a large fistula. It has to be dealt with before any kind of reversal of my colostomy can be done.

When Dr. M. called me, his idea was to insert glue into

the fistula and stitch it closed, have it healed so I can see how that works to proceed with my reversal. Dr. A. and Dr. M. feel this is a good idea. As I'm telling Dr. S. and we are speaking, he is amazed at this. He is smiling and says, "GLUE! Well, why not? Let's proceed!"

Modern medicine! His only concern is that I'm on Keytruda and dealing with my immune system. Will this foreign matter be a concern? I have to ask this question to both Dr. A. and Dr. M.

My Keytruda takes about 40 minutes, then I go home. Dr. A. has left a message on my answering machine. I return his call and he will have to call me back. Phone tag.

Waiting, I'm thinking all about this glue idea and I'm getting very excited. This whole procedure, I felt God had His hands on. I have felt God in my life, bringing me to brighten every day I am on earth. I keep telling myself, "God's timing, not mine." I have to keep reminding myself of this so much, because we (as humans) are in this world by hours, days, minutes, and seconds. God is in the blink of an eye. I am hopeful and energized to be with such a group of doctors who care about me—this human, God's child—to see me succeed, to be cancer free. Be back to me. Thank You, God.

Dr. S. and I finish my appointment. I asked him about my Xarelto (blood thinner). How much longer will I be on this drug? When does it become time to stop taking it? We talk and decide to have me test the waters. I'll stop it for 3 weeks, have a blood test at my next appointment, and see where the results are. This test tells me if I'm in the stage of being a blood clot patient. If my test comes back good, I don't need Xarelto. If it comes back bad, then back on Xeralto I go. I'm good with that.

My heart feels good about this. I don't want to take medications. I'm asking God for His help in my being a good go without Xarelto.

I guess we all need to get up and move more, like exercise (which I despise). God knows me, He knows me best. I lean on Him to be my Guide and Savior. Thank You, God, for being here for me. I will do/try my best to get this body of mine from needing Xarelto.

This is all good news! I'm excited. "THANK YOU, GOD."

72

Today is Friday.

I woke up feeling exhausted. I had a dream. As my dreams go: vivid, engulfing, enlightening, and calming.

I dreamed I was with Dr. A. and Dr. M.! We were talking about my fistula and my surgery. Setting things up to have this procedure done. All things were in place and we're getting ready to do procedure. We were laughing and happy. Everyone was on the same page. We all know how to proceed. Things are moving forward. We were ready to put me to sleep and start to cut. Then I woke up.

I knew God had given me this dream to calm me and know this is the correct way to proceed, with this correction of my fistula. I am confident and happy to move forward.

Thank You, God. You are so good. Thank You for easing my nerves and calming my heart. You always know the way to give me the strength to move forward.

Have the surgery done! Today's Friday the 13th, and it's a good day. Smiles all around. I'm happy, calm, and know this will be perfect.

73

Today starts the first part of my fistula journey. I received a call from Dr. M. My surgery is scheduled for August 3, 2018, at 12:45pm at Sinai Hospital, Baltimore. He will do a colonoscopy type of procedure: fill in the fistula pocket with glue, fuse the tissue together, and stitch it closed. Same day surgery, in and out. Great news. I'm confident.

Part 2: Today, I'll go have my pre-op tests: EKG, blood work, physical. I go to my primary, Dr. SB. She is another doctor on my team. Dr. SB is a doctor l have been seeing for many years, as my primary doctor. I explain to her what Dr. M. is going to do and she also is amazed. Says, "Well, let's get this done!" So my physical is performed, and I move on to the EKG and blood work. I'm always glad when blood work is finished. My veins are very small, and they often roll and flatten, and of course they do this to me. We have to get a more experienced nurse to do this work. One shot and she has it. Thank You, God. Blood drawn, check. I'm on my way. My arm hurts, as always, but it's over. Next to EKG: 5 minutes and it's finished. done. I'm out the door and on my way home.

I get home and my phone rings. It's Dr. A. checking on me to see if my surgery is scheduled. We talk for a few moments. He is also happy with this type of procedure. All of my doctors are in agreement with this procedure: Dr A., Dr. S., Dr. SB., and Dr. M., who will be doing this procedure. It's calming to know my team agrees.

I'm very confident and calm as we move forward. We are one team and have been on this 3 year journey. All want the best for me in one accord with each part they play, to my full result: being healed of cancer.

God has allowed me the wonderful team and their expertise. They all have God's blessing of hands to heal and those hands have been bestowed upon me...

Eight amazing hands laid upon me, this human, God's angel! For God's work to be performed. Thank You, God, for picking me. I am blessed to be a child of the greatest God in our universe. Thank You. I love You, my God.

So many prayers to help me heal and become cancer free. Only a special God with His human children could perform such a miracle, and I am that miracle.

Now we wait for August 3rd. Happy and wide smiles.

August 1, Wednesday

My day started at 6:30am. They see a blip in my EKG. Now I'm sent to a cardiologist, 2 days before my surgery. They rush to get me in. It's an 8:30am appointment. I enter the office and no one is there yet. At 9am, they show up, jeezzzzz! This doctor is nice, kind, all good. Never have seen him before. He explains why I'm here, explains everything to me. I have a blip (have had it for years, yes, I know about this). Says it's just a blip in the electron pulsing, my valves. Nothing to worry about. Great, I'm on my way. Thanks. He'll send the results over to Dr. M. Great. I'm gone.

Now off to my Keytruda infusion. Today is the day I find out if I can be off Xarelto for good, or if I must go back on it. I had to take Xarelto for a couple of blood clots back in 2016. The results are in. No more Xarelto! My percentages are down! Perfect! On Xarelto, my percentage was at 5%, now it is down to a 2%. Thank You, God. Today is Heaven. I mean, when you get great news and the outcome is you won't have to take a medication anymore, it is nirvana. Thank You, God.

There is a 2% chance I will get blood clots. I'm so excited. NO MORE XARELTO!

My Keytruda infusion went well. Thirty minutes this time and I'm on my way. See my ladies in 3 weeks! The nurses are all so great at the center. Without them, this would be a very hard thing to go through. They really help us cancer patients. They calm us and make us smile and laugh. It's almost fun to be here and have all their support. Thank you, ladies!

74

Friday, August 3, 2018. My glue the Fistula Day. Part 1 to
my reversal.

Only God's hands could make this happen. God has put the correct hands in place for me to grow, heal, be a cancer survivor. Thank You, God. You are my strength, my love, my life. I'm getting all my pre-op done. Waiting my turn. We are an hour behind; it's 1:30pm. I'm told I'm next. My S O and I say our I love you's and see you soon's.

Here we go. Time to go to sleep. Out I go.

I wake up in recovery. It has been a 2 hour surgery. I feel sore and achy, but good. Dr. M. comes and talks to me. S O is there, thankful he can hear what I would miss. Dr. M. says, "I have cleaned, glued, fused (had to burn my tissue together as I was so burned by radiation), and stitched you." Three stitches and I'm closed. Fistula repair done.

Dr. M. says all went well, and he hopes it stays closed. I know it will, as God used his hands to perform this miracle, and it is another miracle. Only God, my God has the power to bring this forth and make this happen. Thank You, God, again and again!

I'm released. We are on our way home. A 2 hour ride home for rest/recoup/healing! No driving for a week. Just rest and heal. My poor ass! What a challenge to me and the doctors, but not to God. This is part of God's plan for me. I will get through this. Another hard part, but also another miracle. As my doctors said, "Who thought glue would work?"

I know in my heart and my being, it has, and it will. Thank You, God, for giving me the conscience to feel great about this surgery. To feel relaxed, sure, and calm. Only by Your love for me, can this be possible. Thank You, God.

Not saying this isn't painful. It's healing pain and I will be glad when it is over. Move and sit, sit and move. That is the plan. Smile and love the sun. Comfort in my day. Thank you, cardinals, my bird friends; your visits are a welcome site and give much comfort. Male and female sit in my window to look at me. They are God's angels sent to comfort me in my healing. Thank you, red birds, I know who you are. Thank you.

75

Day 4 after surgery

I'm hurting today. Really hurting. It's painful. When you have pain, you have nerve endings that are working. So this pain is a form of comfort. It means I have nerve endings. My bowel track woken up to feel this pain. Pain means healing, healing means pain. So this pain, healing is a welcome. I will work through this pain and welcome this healing. Thank You, God. You are so good to me and I thank You for my so many miracles. Please keep them coming. I am ready.

Day 10 after surgery

In my healing, doing better every day. I still hurt, but not as bad. Long drives are out. My butt can't handle sitting for long periods of time. It's all in the healing.

Today, I felt God used me in speaking again. One of

my neighbors saw me and stopped to ask how I have been doing. I shared the breakdown of my journey. I'm thankful that God is using me to show His grace and fulfillment of my life. My miracles are very large, and *I know God wants me to talk about them to everyone, as long as they ask.* Many do. My mouth keeps running and doing my best to give glory to God! God's team of healers in my life is a miracle. That God has given to me, this human, my need to speak is grand. People are so kind to listen. Most do agree that my life is a miracle and the glory belongs to God! How great is that.

I only want to show God's glory, strength, and power. Hoping all the time that these people feel the power God's words have.

Today, I am seeing Dr. SB. to talk about my blood work. I have had hypothyroid since my first bout with cancer in 1995. Chemo made this hypo happen as a side effect. In my heart, I know it's going to be better. My blood pressure is perfect, 120/68. How much better is that? Again, thank You, God. My heart rate is 63, so I'm in good shape. Dr SB. walks in and says, "You look fantastic! Your skin, coloring, whole being looks very healthy!" I say, "Thank you, I really feel great. Really, good, healthy."

She says my thyroid is lower and we need to lower my Synthroid medication; it's making my stats crazy. Perfect, I knew that this was going to happen! I knew this was why she wanted to see me. Another one of God's miracles, gifts to me. My whole being wants to be off all medications!

One of my greatest goals is to get my body back to 100%, where I know God also wants me to be. We have talked and God has told me; we are on the same path of goodness.

Thank You, my God. Your glory be praised, and glory to You in heaven. Thank You for "PICKING ME" to be one of Your children to show Your glory and Your love for all of us here on earth. I will do my best to be a voice You use to show the grace and the glory of You, my God. Thank You.

76

Today is a day of blessings. To thank God for His everlasting grace. I just heard of two people I know who are hurting: one who is going through a tough trial, and one who has cancer. They both are God's children.

I pray:

Grant them Your grace, dear Lord. Give them peace, their wishes. You know their hearts and minds. You hold them in the palm of Your hands. Give them people to help and share kindness. See them through, in Jesus' name, I grant these and lift them up.

Thank You, Lord, for making me able and willing to pray, to understand heartache and pain.

You have given me balance in my life, and challenge. Both of which have been mentally and physically tiresome. In all, You have taught me to be thankful and feel the grace You have bestowed on me, to give to others, who may need a lift to grace. I try to show You are a God of trust and encouragement. That I am very grateful for. You have also taught moving forward is necessary and part of balance. Thank You for allowing me to see these gifts, to share what I can in Your name.

You have proven to me so many times that God's love is perfect, even when humans are not. Thank You. You have told me that this book is not about me, it is all about You: God Almighty, Creator of heaven and earth, all things big and small, great and wonderful, happy and sad, so mankind may see Your glory, power, strength, delight. Thank You for opening my eyes, in hopes that others will do the same and learn to love You more and more each day.

My thought for now is:

"Laughter is the best healer. I guess the joke is on all of us."

We all need to find our own laughter and really laugh. We all need to look at ourselves and have a great laugh. If we can laugh at ourselves, we have everyone else beat. That is called balance.

Thank You, God.

77

Today is Keytruda day again. Every 3 weeks. Don't know how long, but as long as it takes, I'll be on Keytruda.

I'm feeling wonderful, clean, clear, healthy. That is where I am today. Dr. S. is happy and smiling for me. We have been working on me for 3 years and God's grace is shining through. It has been all hard work. Not easy, scary, to know 18 months ago, I had three (yes, three) weeks to live. That, my friends, is reality!

Confirmation that life is short. You are your best advocate. You need your best you. Be in charge. Don't let others rule you. You have a heart, LOVE. You have a brain, STUDY. Complete your tasks. Earn your life, your way. Make this journey yours. Get help, but this adventure is always yours. *You need to complete your own life.* God is there to guide, respect, and encourage that. Use these tools to bring forth your best YOU.

God is my go to. When I am troubled, confused,

cautious, lonely, crying, hopeful, hopeless; whatever my
challenge, l have to go talk to my Lord. All can see that He
has pulled me through so many trials and troubles! With
each one, I have come back out more solid than before.
Stronger, yes, but also with more balance. I encourage
balance.

So many days, my equilibrium has been off. I now
realize it was the universe telling me to stop and look for
my balance, to move forward. Wow, even I get moved by
these words. I am learning to keep them close to my heart
and brain. To use them daily. To grow in thought and
wonder for my everlasting, in this human life. Thank
You, God.

By Him, all things have been made possible.

My being, You made possible. My heart, You taught to
love. Also respect my heart to be aware, of those not
worthy of my heart and those who take advantage. Again,
BALANCE. As I must do the same to others. BALANCE.
Kindness in my words, my stature, my wholeness. It is an
everyday gift, lessons to learn.

Thank You, God. "YOU PICKED ME."

78

This week had been a different type of interesting. The moon and Mars meet. It was too hazy to see this happen. I guess you could call it the pull, the magnetic force, this happening, and it has given me strange happenings! Things felt to be easy going. They should fall into place. But normal everyday wonders became mixed up, eventful, crazy, working in reverse. It showed me that our world is not just revolving; our world is made of push and pulls, and we are the powerful force that must move around it. To stay focused. Gravity is pulling us to do better. Magnetic, it's pulling us around.

God's forces are in charge and we must revolve around this wonderful earth, God's world. I have learned we revolve around the world. The world does not revolve around us. We are not in control of this. God is the power who controls this revolving. The sooner we learn these lessons, the better understanding we are allowed to have.

This is God's world, and we have been allowed to live, breathe, consume, teach, learn, and respect here. God has given us free will, *and He will never let us forget that*. We can make up our minds and change our minds. We are accountable for our actions. Always our actions.

It's Friday, and it has been a crazy week. It has taught me a lot: to be patient, think level headed, not to react, go slow. Remember the end game and work it out. Make it positive, always positive—a lesson I am continually having to work toward. Taking my energy to get to my best finish. I did, and when I realized I needed to, all fell into place for me. My better balance. Things worked out and I was able to finish my projects, goals, wishes. I listened toward the energy and balance You were trying to get me to understand. Thank You, God.

I hope that in my endeavor to pursue, I am able to help others do the same. We need to believe God is in control and only wants our best to perform our duties. To move through this earth, in our human form, and be constant. To put away our fear, our "NO" selves, and our "I'M IN CHARGE" selves. To get to the point of greatness to understand the universe, our God's planet, earth. To enjoy the beauty in our everyday life and see how the sunshine brings smiles to our faces. To see growth in creatures, flowers, trees, everything around us.

Our waters, that are all around us, to prosper and dwell in. Again, our balance. This lesson I have been taught and am still learning. I also wish all to be taught. Thank You, God, for allowing me, your human angel, to be blessed with all these gifts, and try to help others with all these and this blessing.

Thank You for my crazy week to learn from and making all this possible through You! In Jesus' name, Amen.

79

This week is a hard week. So many things to go through. I know it may sound trivial, but in my shoes, it's not. Nor do I want anyone to wear them.

The whole east coast is preparing for Hurricane Florence. *God please protect all,* grant them safety, strength, and preparedness.

This week is also the anniversary of 9/11, September 2001, a time for all Americans: strength, love, togetherness, family, and friends.

I have my own challenges this week.

Wednesday: Keytruda day. All went well. I had my infusion. Spent my 40 minutes being juiced. Didn't have to see Dr. S. Thank You, God, for allowing me Keytruda. For my body accepting the juice, and for it as part of my maintenance program to prevent cancer. A cancer that has tried to kill me many times. It is only Your perfect plan, Your pleasure of me, that I am standing, breathing, existing, living to this day.

Thursday: my 5th, yes 5th, barium enema test! These tests are strenuous on my body. They hurt and are invasive. I have had them, and they are the knowledge needed to tell the doctors how my bowel/colon is healing. Healing so we can get me reversed from my colostomy bag. It's been a long healing time. I am so ready for my reversal to happen. I sit on the edge of my seat every time I have these tests. The outcome has all been good, and we have moved forward with much progress. I thank my God for His grace and knowledge, providing for my well-being. We have all learned so much during this part of my recovery.

We wait till the results are in. Drs. M./A./S. get to see how I have healed and how we proceed to the next page on my path of reversal. This test will tell if doing my August 3rd surgery held and if all doctors are happy with these results. I'm sure this won't happen for many days; it is Thursday, and most times, nothing happens on the weekends. Sit, wait, and continue praying.

I have an exam with Dr. A. next Friday, September 21 (also my birthday). As nurse N. put it, "It will be your birthday exam!" Yay!

80

Monday. Nothing yet, no word, no calls. We move to the next daily life developments. I'm feeling sorrow, I just heard of a fellow cancer victim's passing (the one I had told you about). I knew he was doing poorly and it was just a matter of time. He passed on Saturday. I learned today.

This is hard coping, feeling that cancer (again) took a person back home to God. We humans have the discomfort of human life and human pain. We will get over this pain. I have learned that the passing of someone needs to be celebrated. They have lived to the fullest and life is a celebration. With death, we need to celebrate them going home to the glorious life of God. To the heavens! To be with our Majestic God. He is now one of our angels and will hold us near to him. That is the strength and power that God has taught me. I believe in this. My belief has gotten stronger as time and cancer has been a part of my daily life. Blessings to you, new angel of God. Praise to Your glory, my God above. Thank You, God.

81

I t's Friday, September 21, 2018.
Today is my birthday! Praise You, God. I've gotten through another year to celebrate my life. To celebrate another year through cancer. To celebrate my day of being born. My day to see Dr. A. My exam day. My results for my 5th barium enema test. Is the fistula there? Is it gone? Did my surgery work? Did the GLUE work? In my heart, I know my prayers were answered. Do I get my reversal? It's not "IF," it's "WHEN." It's only a 20 minute drive. I'm looking forward to this exam, as I have been waiting for 18 months for this.

Another 8 in my life. I love anything to do with the number 8: 18, 28. And 3. Also 7. As they say, these are my numbers. As my birthday is the 21st, and 2 + 1 = 3. These are all happy numbers for me. I was born at 8:28am, and my children are 8, 18, 28. How can all this be wrong? Again, thank You, God. Waiting my turn, called in, and Dr. A. and nurse N. walk in the room. We always hug and smile. I notice he is really smiling! Smiling a very good sign. Now I know it's good news. I knew in my heart and soul this was going to be good. I still had to wait for this to be confirmed.

Dr. A. shows me the report of my Barium test. He says, "THE FISTULA IS GONE! There are no signs of the fistula being there. My bowel track is healed. We are cleared to do your reversal." I'm smiling, my S O is smiling, smiles all around. These are glorious words to our ears. We have been yearning for this day for months. On my birthday, the greatest gift has been delivered. God's plan is almost complete. I can have my surgery; I can be reversed! My colostomy will be no more.

Who is ever happy to have surgery? Well, today I am! Happy birthday, you received your wish. God has granted you your wish.

We talked about this upcoming surgery and decided it can be after October 3, 2018. Two months after my August 3rd surgery that fixed my fistula. All enough time for healing.

Dr. A. examines me and is very happy with my progress, says everything feels smooth and clear. So I'm good to go. We hug and I say my thank you's to him and nurse N. We say good-byes. He says he will see me at surgery.

On Monday, I call Dr. A.'s office to schedule my date for my reversal of my colostomy surgery. This is exciting. It has been a long wait. We make arrangements for Monday, October 22, 2018, at 10am. She pencils me in. I'm excited, elated, all the above words that can't be expressed.

God has brought me through this very long journey.

We have conquered hills and valleys together. I have shared my love for Him and His love for me. We are together in this circle and we are rising as power. Thank You, God. Thank You for having my back. Thank You for seeing me through. Thank You for loving me.

82

Tuesday, 2 weeks before my colostomy surgery. I have to go see my primary doctor, Dr. SB. She will do my pre-op exam, blood work, EKG , physical—basically check me out for the all good to have surgery. All my tests I had for my Keytruda this month are adequate for my pre-op. My blood work is great, my EKG, and all information done. She will send all to Dr. A.'s office. All looks good and I'm on my way. Easy and done.

I return home and get a call from Dr. A.'s office. They ask if I have had my pre-op yet. I say, "I just did." As I am talking, they are getting my paperwork through fax. Great. Check. Hang up.

An hour goes by and I received another call from Dr. SB. My EKG will be 3 days out of date and I need to go have a new one. I go back the next day, Wednesday. Now to wait for surgery.

83

Wednesday, the following week, 10/10/18. I have an appointment with L.W. She is going to help me figure out where I am! Daughter #1 and I are going together. She is a spiritual advisor. God has brought us together and made this possible. I'm encouraged to hear what she has to say. This is therapy, this is healing, this is knowledge.

What a wonderful surprise. Daughter #1 and I are happy to listen to L.W. Her knowledge of our past, present, now. Many things are spot on. We slowly move forward into more information. I'm learning many things and can't believe I'm hearing the words being said! I'm sorry I can't reveal all of our session, but the shock is beyond my ears. It was a great session. I'm sad, happy, scared. Now I have to process what my ears have heard, and my brain can't comprehend. I'm stunned by some truths and saddened by some others. All I can think is, God please help me!

Help me to understand these words and process this information. My heart hurts, my body is crying. I must seek my God. I must feel His power to see me through. I may not be making sense, but I know I have to find my bearings .

My balance is to come to grips with this information. Daughter #1 says she's okay, and I need to believe in myself, process, and accept.

Please, God, help me. I feel lost, lonely, alone, ashamed. I know only by Your grace can I free my brain and my heart. Only by Your love can I forgive myself. I'm so tired, my energy won't let me sleep. I need to sleep. To rest, to restore, to renew. Hold me, my God. Hug me, be my balance. Be my strength. I have to leave this alone and move forward, get past this heart pain. This selfish past. Move to this future of greatness. Please help me, my God. Your perfect wisdom and motivation to move me forward. Thank You, my God. I need You to love me, move past this pain. Thank You, my God. Thank You.

Another night without a lot of sleep. I'm tired and my head is still reeling. Some anger is setting in. Yes, I guess it's going through the steps of realization and it sucks! I only wait for calm to set in and I'll know I'm coping. This human body is feeling this anguish and pain of earth. *I need my spirit to grow and my human diminish.* It will in time. I have God's time, not human time. Snap your fingers, God, and let me see Your light. Then I will know relief in my heart! I am starting in my heart. I know it's there. In my heart, I know the end. All will be powerful and clear. I will be back to balance again. Thank You, God.

Thank You for holding me up. Watching my back. Loving my heart and loving me. Thank You for allowing me to understand that You "PICKED ME."

84

This week is a week of wait. My heart is aching, my heart hurts. It's been a rough time trying to get my mind, body, soul, being all in sync. Dealing with last week's information and trying to make my brain comprehend the information. Being shocked and stymied is crippling.

Trying to feel balance, preparing for my upcoming surgery. I need for my head to be on straight, even, complete. I know this will take time to do. I'm hoping God, my God, will encourage me to be patient and open minded to be able to use my prayers and strength to come to balance. Sometimes things don't happen directly or immediately, but we all have to allow this process to happen. I am, and I want a resolution for my information. I will get the help I need to understand all of this. I'm confident about this. It is necessary for my being to move forward and be okay. To learn everything that has happened is okay. Moving forward for the good of all through Christ Almighty. I know this in my heart and my reality.

This puzzle is starting to fit! Thank You, God, My Savior.

Only a few more days and I'm praying more details to be revealed as understood. I see an end to this path and a glory to behold through all these trials. God be with us, and also with you. Thank You. Yes, thank You.

85

October 22, 2018, Monday, surgery day! Reversal of my colostomy. At Sinai Hospital, Baltimore. 11am.

My anticipation is so high. I hope I'm not putting myself in a tailspin. I know God has been preparing me for this day for months. It has been 18 months, and living with a colostomy may be the hardest thing ever, may even top cancer, but... maybe not. This journey has been a long, but knowledgeable one. The things I have learned about myself, about people, about God.

God promised He wouldn't leave me; He has kept that promise. He has allowed me peace, guidance, patience, and much love. I have learned to love myself before all else. I have learned to put myself first. I am important. I am real. I am perfect. To know I make mistakes, break my rules, promises, hurt, ignore, all the life lessons.

That is my goal in this life: to be as good as God wants me to be.

I had my type and screen (blood work). Have all my

pre-op completed. It's now 11:30am and Dr. A. is still in another surgery. All okay, it's good. By 12:30pm, I've seen all the operating room DR's, and we are a go. They put me to sleep and surgery is being performed.

I'm waking up in recovery. Late afternoon. Surgery was about 3 hours. I'm resting and getting ready to go to my room. I'm staying in the hospital a few days, in my room, which is private. Really nice. S O and daughter #2 are here. I'm in my bed. All monitors are hooked up and I'm on/off sleeping. They go to get something to eat, so I can sleep. I'm really feeling good. Not a lot of pain. Not much uncomfortable. It's gonna be a long night. Daughter #2 goes home and S O is staying with me. On/off all night, waken up for vitals, blood work, checking on me and medications. This goes on throughout the first night. At 6:30am, Dr. A.'s team of doctors, residents, comes in, checks me. I'm doing good. I'm in a hospital. The routine starts.

I tell the team, "I want to get up and walk. I need to get out of this bed and move." They say, "okay." A little while later, I have my catheter removed so I can get up and move, pee on my own. Move my body. Relief. On the ward, SO and I take our stroll down the corridor, 10 to 15 minutes at a time, slow, relaxed, but moving. We decide to do this every hour; what else are you going to do in the hospital? Daughter #2 shows up and she decides to stay behind, all strolling in the hallways, in one, out the other, hour after hour. All are surprised I'm doing so well! It's a good day. Daughter #2 has been here all day. She and S O decide it's time to go get food. I'm on a liquid diet only; no food for me. It's now Tuesday. I am starving. I haven't had food since Friday before my surgery! It's time to send Daughter #2 home; its late. She has a long drive. Kisses and hugs, thank you, and she leaves. She has been a real charm, bringing food for S O and her to eat. Thank you, Daughter #2! I Love You...

The night routine begins, same as last night. Really, no sleeping in the hospital! Every morning at 6:30am, the team comes in and checks on me. Today is Wednesday. They remove my bandages, take my binder off, and everything looks good. Incision looks good. They ask me some questions. I tell them, "I am hungry! When can I have food? It has been 5 days with only broth and liquids in my stomach." They say, "You must fart for your bowels to start!" I laugh and say, "I don't fart; I burp, I'm a burper." They are happy with my progress, say I'm doing great moving and walking.

They say, "You are doing so well, maybe we will let you go home today!" Okay, that works for me! I have to see Dr. A.'s associate, Dr. F. If she feels I am good, maybe I can go. "We will order you some food and see how that works on your stomach." My answer is "PERFECT." I would like to be released and eat. So we move forward.

It's about 12:30pm. Dr. F. comes in and she is very surprised with my energy. I'm moving and really feel good. We talk and she says against her better judgement, she will release me this afternoon after I have food and keep it down. I still haven't farted, but I am burping; as I said, I don't fart, I burp. I know passing gas is my main concern. I get that, but without food, it's not going to happen. I end up getting my food: chicken noodle soup, toast, apple sauce, and a banana. All soft and easy to digest (the goal). Around 3:30pm, I am released. Going home! We leave the hospital relieved.

We arrive home around 7pm. We had to stop to get my prescription. Now to have something to eat and go to bed. I'm very tired. A long ride takes a lot out of you. I'm on laxatives and stool softeners; we need to get my bowels moving. I've had food and a bumping car ride, that should help! My goal is to rest, eat, fart, poop, and no straining. Eighteen months of no use, we don't want to injure my bowel/put strain on my tract.

It's Thursday morning. I didn't sleep well; my nerves got the best of me. Worry is not a good feeling. I was worried about not farting and pooping. I prayed all night. Thanking God for all these trials and asking for His love in helping me to fart and poop. Finally, around 8:30am, my butt allowed me to fart, and fart I did! Around 2pm that afternoon, my body allowed me to poop. Food and calm have helped me to relax. Along with my prayers to God. A big sigh of relief. Both happened and my body feels so happy to respond.

Thank You, God, for yet another miracle. I am reversed, I am alive. Now the days forward will be to keep my bowels moving. Allow my body to learn again how to function through its normal everyday.

God told me:

"Come to Me with open arms. My arms will always be there. Come to Me and hold Me tight. My arms will never fail." This verse is my strength, my hope, and my power. God gave this to me, and I'm proud to share these words of God.

Think how good God really is. He's funny, He's gentle,

He's logical, and He's real. He makes me want to be a better person, make better decisions. Help others with the knowledge He has provided to me. To share and pass it around. Our God, this amazing God, is the only way to go through my life. I had to learn this and as you have read, *it wasn't easy! As I look back, it was all worth it.* I needed all these trials to learn and become strong, able, correct. Without them, who knows... That I don't want to think about. Thank You, God. You love me....

86

Monday, 1 week since my reversal surgery

I really am feeling good. I'm on my way to being back to me, before cancer and all these surgeries to keep me alive. It's amazing to think back in years. All this started again in June 2015. One small tumor turned into a large one in 60 days. Four summers and about 1220 days/nights. I can't even think of the minutes/seconds that have passed. It gives me pause to reflect on this journey of becoming a whole functioning human again. Today is also labs, blood work, for my infusion on Wednesday. Keytruda infusion. All goes well.

Wednesday (October 31, 2018, Halloween)

It's also 21 year anniversary for S O and me! WOW, this is just amazing. We have made it through. I am reversed.

God has allowed us to honor our anniversary and enjoy our time together.

Keytruda was a laughing trip. Everyone in the Cancer Center was in such good spirits! All us cancer patients were laughing and enjoying our infusions. Happy Halloween.

Friday

We went to our usual hometown restaurant. Saw all the local people/friends. They wished me well, happy to see S O and me. Glad all went well with my reversal surgery. Were very happy for me to be there and it was fun just to be out and about.

Even with all the humor, this week was not all peaches and cream. I learned a friend died of cancer, another is terminal, another was having cancer surgery, another this and that. For all my happy miracles, and I am so thankful for them. Others are not so lucky. Cancer doesn't pick who wins, cancer just picks. God picks who wins and who is to go home to Him. My love of my God has gotten me through every day. His love for me holds me tight and keeps me wanting more.

I will do my best to be an angel of light to shine for God. To show others how truly awesome my God is. His power to heal and do these miracles in my life. Today, tomorrow, yesterday, always. I'm not for a second saying I know all the reasons "GOD PICKED ME," but I do know He did. I WILL do my best to show how He has been my guiding light.

These past 10 days have also been trying. One of my

family members has had an aneurysm, frontal lobe, brain bleed. The same day as my surgery, 10/22/2018. Our family is holding it together. We only want the best. I.C.U. is not a place you want to spend your days/weeks. Our God has again proven His love. With a 30% chance of survival, we are doing "GOOD!" Good is the word for this week; last week it was "OKAY." So we have been upgraded to "GOOD."

In week 2, we have seen some setbacks. The doctors said they can't figure out why he hasn't had a stroke yet. But we can. We have had many people praying. This, too, is in God's hands. This, too, is God's timing. This, too, is God's power. Time and wait. God's time. God's wait. God will prevail. Thank You, God. Thank You.

87

Monday. It has 2 weeks since my reversal. I'm doing great. Healing well. Moving my bowels, farting, functioning normal. I'm in no pain. Of course, lifting and doing many things are out for now, as healing is the goal.

This week has been a painful (heart) week. Some interesting happenings, the only way I can describe it.

Our family member who had the aneurysm is doing "GOOD," as doctors say. We had an interesting experience. Someone was trying to bring evil into this household. God would not have any of this. God brought His angel forth to reveal our knowledge and confirmation.

God brings/uses other people who are believers. Helping with reassuring us. Those who need the hand of God in situations of this kind. This gentleman came to fix a stopped up drain in the bathroom shower. He heard our conversation. He asked if he could pray! Of course, we said "YES." So he did. He prayed a beautiful prayer to cleanse this home! To bring God's light to shine. As he was praying, the light and spirit of God shone in our hearts. A feeling of comfort and warmth. Thank you to him! Power rose up and made this situation a peaceful and calming one. This house went back to a godly home and evil was cast away.

Maybe it seems unreal to many. To us, in our love of God, it is very real. Thank You, God, for providing this angel of mercy—cleansing this house and cleansing our souls for the better. Helping us with clarity and under-standing of Your powerful knowledge. This home is calm.

Our family member was also having a bad day that same time. They will have many days with an aneurysm (a brain bleed with swelling). After his prayer, they, too, got to the bottom of that bad day and fixed it! To become a better one. Not to say bad days don't happen naturally, but this was not a natural thing. We are happy for these results. Pray and wish only comfort and healing. This time will be long, and this healing will be slow. We know it will have God's hands in all. Thank You, thank You, God.

88

Today marks 3 weeks since my reversal surgery. All is good. All is great. I'm feeling excellent. Really, better than great. I'm still having to remember the past 18 months, with my colostomy bag. Still feeling the energy of knowing that this colostomy was what kept me alive. That this time was needed to have my body heal and become cancer free. That this surgery was a necessary part of growth and knowledge, to be part of my journey through this life. I also learned that sometimes you have to go through fear to get to calm. To go through pain to get to freedom. All these emotions are part of life's journey. In all, we MUST remember to contour good. That there can also be bad. All through my journey to be free from cancer, my heart kept telling me GOOD would prevail. That this long journey would have a peaceful end. "GOD'S TIME, NOT HUMAN TIME."

This has also given me reflecting time. To take these past few years and realize this has been a better learning experience. To get to know me, this human person. This person to love. Love of thy self. "To accept, not expect." Oh, that's a hard one. I am flawed. I am not perfect. I am God's child. I know I keep talking of human life, human person, human beings.

That is what we are here on God's earth. We have a choice. We have freedom. We have free will. That is called human.

To say we can change is human. But we will make mistakes. We will make choices. We have that freedom to do so. We also have that freedom to change. To become a better me, we, us. All through the love of self, with the help of God, if we so choose. What a concept to behold. God wants us for better. To make the hard choice for our salvation. To conquer that journey that becomes a reality. To see the good in all, even the bad, evil, challenge. To accept hardship to reach encouragement, success, freedom.

These past 3 weeks have had many challenges. Some I wish I could have wished away. I am sad that I learned information I had to accept. Some of life's pain and hurt to become a happier end. To bring the reality that we are all human. But, again, God's children.

This is my belief, I know. It calms me. I hope you as my readers have a sense of calm, as well. This book is about life with God in it. I choose that. That choice was made in me when I was a little girl. As a young girl, I knew it was there, but what was my mission to find? I feel I've succeeded in that mission. I brought forth my being, soul, and life. It has been a rocky one. It has been a hard one. It has been a good one. .

Loads of knowledge was instilled in me. Sometimes not the sharpest tool in the shed! Always looking at the sun to provide my balance. Sometimes sitting back and soaking up my life's knowledge. Trying to learn from my mistakes. Trying to avoid pain, heartache, loss. To challenge myself and to learn to celebrate every day. No one promised me a piece of cake. Just the opposite. My trials, my journey, and my life had to be my choices.

Guidance was there, if I chose. Learning was there, if I wanted to learn. Knowledge was at my fingertips, if I so wanted. But they were my choices to make: good, bad, or indifferent. It has always been on me to make these decisions. Learning many hard lessons. Always on me. We can't blame someone else for our own choices. We must own this choice for ourselves. Make the hard decisions and accept the end result. As I have chosen to do this, God became my best friend. I know in my heart I could always count on God to give me the truest answer, reality, and encouragement. I was disappointed by many humans. I'm sure I was a disappointment, too. But through all of life's accomplishments, I would say, "It has been a wonderful life."

I'm also happy to have learned a few steps in the future. I also need to stay in the here and now, to make every day count. Make every day a success. To encourage my life and human contacts with the best l can be. To make my God/my Almighty feel He picked the correct person to bring forth His lessons. Progress to fulfill this dream as angel to human. As this Book is titled "GOD PICKED ME."

89

THIS SPECIAL GIFT

This was a very hard week. My friend T.C. and I were cancer friends. In 2015, when I first found out my cancer had returned after 20 years, I was having a hard time dealing with this. Then I went to the fish market to get some scallops; as fish, scallops was good food for me. I learned T.C. owned the market and was also going through his own battle with brain cancer. Had surgery and started chemotherapy. We were on the same track.

We were discussing our treatments. Time went on and I regularly visited the fish market. T.C. and I talked about our concerns, our treatments, and shared our information. We knew each other, but now cancer had given us a power link. We became connected. When I found out in 2016 that my cancer was gone, T.C. was doing well and his cancer was gone, too.

As 2016 came, we were both good. Keeping up with

our regime and doing our every day. I went through chemo during the summer of 2016, and T.C. was still on his regime of cancer healing pills chemo. We stayed connected just to keep up with each other's progress. I lost my hair, T.C. did not. We laughed, but we were still in the clear. Every day moved on and we did our daily life. Didn't see each other much, but T.C. would call every once in a while to check on me.

In 2017, my cancer returned with an aggressive vengeance. T.C. and I talked and he just found out his brain cancer returned. He needed another brain surgery. I was having my bowel, pelvic, and colostomy. I had my surgery, chemo again, and we both were in tough cancer fights. We saw each other again at the fish market, him still working and me healing. It took both of us longer to heal and get back to our everyday routines. T.C. would call every so often to check on me, see how I was doing. Slowly, I was healing. Slowly, T.C. was getting worse. I changed treatments and went to Keytruda in November of 2017. Months passed. We got through 2017, healing slowly.

It soon turned to 2018. Keytruda had me feeling much better. T.C. was on much more treatment, but never gave up, even feeling the effects of it all. Spring came and I got the news my cancer was gone. I was making great progress. I visited T.C. again at the fish market; he was still working, but not doing so well. His cancer had gotten worse, taking its toll on him. He was taking treatments a lot, causing him to not be around so much. I kept missing him on my trips to the fish market. One of the last times I saw him, he was on so many steroids, his treatments, and he was still his happy-going-through-life-self. We joked and laughed. T.C. was a great man. Gentle, kind, and giving. I was thinking I had to get back to see him again.

I had just been to the doctors for another consult that day. That evening, I found out T.C. had passed a few days earlier. I didn't use my gut feeling to get to see him as I had planned. I'm sorry, T.C., that I missed you!

T.C.'s funeral was the other day. Being loved and very popular, everyone came to say good-bye. The church was packed. A good send off to an incredible man. Rest soundly, T.C., you are with God. Your pain is gone, and I know you are one of my angels. Thanks for taking care of me and showing me your bravery. *You will always be in my heart.* Thanks to your family for sharing you with this world. You made an impact, for sure. I will miss you!

I see many cardinals outside my windows. The bright red colored ones! Thank you for your visits. They listen so much to me. Thank you for showing me peace and love in God's world today. I will always enjoy you showing up outside my windows.

SPECIAL GIFT

Today, I said goodbye to another special friend, JAF. He was so empowering, full of life, and a complex man. One very dear hearted one. As I listened to the pastor speak of JAF, it made me feel so grateful for having known him. All the wonderful stories of him, his childhood antics, his charisma and charm. Fun-loving-friend-to-all kind of guy. He had his short falls, as we all do.   JAF was fun and his smile was infectious. His balance of life. He inspired me and many. He knew everyone. Many came to say, not farewell, but see you later. He also had cancer. Bone cancer. JAF was gone in 6 weeks. It was fast, but I am glad he got to live his life full, very full. For 56 years, JAF was and did things his way. I didn't realize I knew him almost half his life. WOW, what a treasure for me.

Thank You, God, for taking him home. I know he is okay. My heart tells me this. He was a force. He made me feel special, even when I was going through my cancer. He would come to see me, tell me how brave I was to go through all the steps of cancer, surgery, chemo, and beyond. *Thank you for your support ,JAF!!* He loved my nails. Always wanted his back and arms scratched. I was always glad to do it. We all laughed and said he was a nail whore. He always wanted more. I loved that about him.

When his cancer got to be far in his body and nothing more could be done, he called. Asked for me to come and rub him. As I did, we talked, and I knew things were not good. He asked many questions, as he knew his outcome before anyone else did. I knew God was taking care of him, just by his calmness and understanding of his own fate. Did he like it? NO, of course not, but did he do all to understand it? Yes, he did. He went to God with an open heart and knowledge as humans could never understand. On 7-11-2019, JAF went home. It was 7-11; this funny guy picked his date. How supreme is that. At least, I think so.

To you, my friend: I'll always see you in my heart, and my nails will never be the same. *When I look at them, it's your face they will remember.* They will miss your back and arms, you will never be forgotten. I see you also in the cardinals around my windows. I know you are here to protect me. Another one of my guardian angels. You came to me at the beach the day after you went home. I had never seen a bright red cardinal, EVER, at the beach. But you came and I knew you were okay. I will miss you, my friend. But I know you are well with God. Thank you, Love you.

Special Thank You

There comes a time in everyone's life that someone special floats in, and if you are lucky, they stay. Sometimes they move on. I have been lucky to have God choose my good friend MFR to stay. We haven't been very close for many years. God made this friendship happen, God made it special. She and I have helped each other in ways that are so special. I can't begin to explain. Only to say, God's hand is so large that only He could have been the one to create this special bond. Thank You, God, Thank you, MFR. You know what you have done and how you have helped. *You said YES when I asked and to do this wonderful job, as it challenges me.* It is a touch of your fingers. Fast and easy to no end.

No thank you will ever be enough. God told me to ask, and you responded. You became my words and put them to paper. Thank you, my friend MFR, I love you.

90

First surgery, 3/27/17

What I said going into surgery:

1. It's okay, that's my crazy daughter. She's the baby!
2. I had to get a big ass scar, but I saved my ass hole.
3. Oh, great, I have 2 asses again: an ass in the front, and an ass in back.
4. Oh, this is just beautiful (looking at my scar).

Second surgery, 9/18/2017

Reattached my anus, again, re-stitched 360 degrees all around, chain stitch.

Third surgery, 8/3/2018

Fistula, glued fistula, fused tissue together, stitched closed.

Fourth surgery, 10/22/2018 (home on 10/24/2018)

Colostomy reversal, must fart and poop, no food 5 days, liquids only. Farted and pooped 10/25/2018 after food and coming home.

91

Encounter #1, August 1982, Pregnant Dream

Y ou are a little girl sitting at the bended knee of Jesus. He's in His white robes, glowing and smiling, telling you, "You will have another child. A girl. She will be fine, always fine, never forget that. Your pregnancy, not so. Many perils, sickness, but remember the baby will always be fine. All the problems are with your human body. It may seem the baby's in stress, but it's your body, not the baby."

She says, "No" to Jesus.

He says, "I will protect them both, and not another pregnancy will happen after this one. But you must accept these terms."

I try to fight Him, but I know I can't. I wake up the next morning and I can't believe I had this dream. I wake up crying and almost paralyzed. I can't move. All I can do is remember the dream.

Encounter #2, May 1993, Ghost Dream

In this dream, I was in my bed, and ghosts were flying all around me, pulling me up toward the ceiling in my bedroom. Above my bed, a big hole was in the ceiling, an opening to go through. The ghost pulled me toward it again and again. Confused, I didn't know what to do. I was getting closer... and closer. I had to make a decision: go through or not.

I soon realized *I had the power* to break away and stop this. I put my hands and feet on the ceiling to stop myself from going through the hole. The ghosts were all through and I was left on all fours.

Next, I woke up in my bed, paralyzed. On my back, I couldn't move my legs, arms, or body. Only my eyes could open; they moved from side to side. *I tried to move*, but I couldn't. In my amazement, I understood my dream. I had to lay quietly. I made a decision to stay alive, deal with *my problems,* and figure it out. It took me 10 minutes before I could move. God gave me a choice to live or die, and I took life!

Encounter #3, October 27, 1995, Cancer Surgery #1

I was coming out of my cancer surgery 1995. My first bout with cancer. I'm in the recovery room. The nurse is waking me up from my sleep, she asks me "Who is Daughter #2 name?" I ask her, "What? She says "Who is Daughter #2 name." I tell her, "She is my 12 year old daughter. She says I kept saying, "Not now Jesus, there is no one to take care of her." I said, "I can't go, I can't die, not now please." Over and over I kept saying this.

Encounter #4, January 2016, Reoccurrence of Cancer

I was dreaming about having been cured of cancer. My dream was that my cancer came back again. This was my 3rd time having this cancer, endometrial and cervical, and it wasn't good. I woke up so scared.

Encounter #5, February 21, 2016, Pirate Dream/Being Chased

I am asleep and I am dreaming, it starts. I was trying to get away from people (mostly men) trying to kill me. I had to climb up, up, up. I was using hook type "J" to pull me up; some were made of animal hooves or rabbit paws. Whatever type, grappling hooks, always a step up to grab to hoist myself up, to get away. As soon as I got up, I found more people coming after me. So I found more J hooks to climb.

One man helped me by putting me on his shoulders and pushing me up. He was a big man, tall, broad shoulders, keeping everyone else away, not wanting to hurt me. It seemed every tier I got to, my efforts had to start again. At one point, I thought I was on a pirate ship and scurrying away, hurrying away from all these people. Another was a cha-cha type of store and I used rails around the ceiling to elude them. But always going up, up, up to the next level.

Finally, I got to the top and saw the hatch cover in the ceiling, like an opening to your attic. I tried to push up the panel, but it wouldn't budge. Scared, I kept pushing harder and harder. Then all of a sudden, I burst out laughing, saying, "God, you are funny," and ending the dream. I was still laughing as I woke myself up from the laughter. As I woke up, I had to get a pen and paper, writing these words: "The door it won't open. God said, 'NO! Your time is not over, get up and go finish your story, I'll tell you when, as you have always known. I love you, my best friend.'"

Encounter #6, October 16, 2016, Eulogy/Obituary Dream

God told me in my dream that I must write my eulogy, my obituary. I got up and did, knowing I wasn't dying. I had to write it down this poem.

I was having a dream one night. God came to me and said these words: "Come to Me, open arms. My arms will always be there. Come to Me and hold Me tight. My arms will never fail." I woke up, I knew I had to write them down. They are compelling and give me strength. Thank You, God.

Encounter #7, December 2017, Book Title Dream

I know I am sleeping, human sleeping. Sleeping and dreaming in my dream. Many things are rushing through my mind, but still know that I know I am asleep. Dreaming within a sleep and dreaming. Trying to figure out what I'm supposed to be doing.

God and I are communicating, though. I knew He was

speaking to me, racing in my mind. I know this, but am trying to make sense of all these thoughts. Much like any other dream, but I know there is significant knowledge I need to understand. Trying to get the process going, to understand, when all of a sudden, I wake up from the intense dream. Woke up in my human dream knowing my answer to all of these thoughts. God gave me the title of the book: *GOD PICKED ME.*

Again, this is so profound, I begin to have tears roll down my cheeks, and I smile. My heart is bursting with joy. I have longed for this, for months. Almost feeling guilty for not having a title. I should already know, God's timing not mine! Again, thank You, God.

Encounter #8, March 20, 2018, Angel Dream

I have this feeling: I'm lying on my right side, covers on, quietly asking, "God, who am I? What is this all about?" I can't move, my body is frozen. *We talk.*

God tells me I'm His angel and I wanted to come to earth to see how humans live. He gives me a choice as to what and how to make this life: hard/easy/so so. He asks for my answer and I say, "HARD." Then hard, it is. I know I'm in God's great presence and doing God's will. Not perfect, not always correct, but I'm 64 years old, trying to be faithful, encouraging, sometimes feeling great, others not understanding cancer, but knowing I must move forward. I asked! Human I am. My godly will. I know God loves me, His eternal blessing.

He tells me He will never leave me, I am not alone, and He will always have my back. Being God's child, trusting His hands, and trusting His love. Beating this human mind, I wake up. Thank You, God, for allowing me (Your angel) *grace and will!*

I remember lying there, and my mind wants to remember every detail. I am not able to move; nothing but my eyes, like I am paralyzed. Still talking, my conversation with God. He knows me, my sense of learning, *my need for HIM.*

So now I must take this encounter, this dream, and realize what I have been given. Take this gift and try to do the best every human can do.

MEET THE AUTHOR

BONNIE J. SCHAAL is a cancer survivor, a mom, a friend, a lover. Her love of finding herself through her love of God has been her biggest accomplishment. She believes that life is a great teacher. Cancer and her survival has brought her to this book. Knowledge, understanding, and truth has been her reward.

Bonnie in various stages of recovery.

Made in the USA
Middletown, DE
20 July 2023